# Building Consensus for a Sustainable Future: Putting Principles into Practice

*Gerald Cormick, Norman Dale, Paul Emond, S. Glenn Sigurdson and Barry D. Stuart*

National Round Table
on the Environment
and the Economy

Table ronde nationale
sur l'environnement
et l'économie

**Canadian Cataloguing in Publication Data**
Main entry under title:
Building consensus for a sustainable future: putting principles into practice
(National Round Table series on sustainable development)
Issued also in French under title: Forger un consensus pour un avenir viable : des principes à la pratique
Includes bibliographical references
ISBN 1-895643-42-2

1. Consensus (Social sciences). 2. Political science — Decision making. 3. Sustainable development — Decision making. 4. Political development. I. Cormick, Gerald  II. National Round Table on the Environment and the Economy (Canada) III. Series.

HM131.B77 1996 302.3
C96-900786-8

This book is printed on Environmental Choice paper containing over 50 percent recycled content including 10 percent post-consumer fibre, using vegetable inks. The coverboard also has recycled content and is finished with a water-based, wax-free varnish.

**National Round Table Series on Sustainable Development**

1.  Pathways to Sustainability: Assessing Our Progress

2.  A Practical Introduction to Environmental Management on Canadian Campuses

3.  Covering the Environment: A Handbook on Environmental Journalism

4.  Sustainable Development: Getting There from Here

5.  Trade, Environment and Competitiveness

6.  Building Consensus for a Sustainable Future: Putting Principles into Practice

Toutes publications de la Table ronde nationale sur l'environnement et l'économie sont disponibles en français.

**National Round Table on the Environment and the Economy**
1 Nicholas St., Suite 1500
Ottawa, Ontario
Canada K1N 7B7
Tel: (613) 992-7189
Fax: (613) 992-7385
E-mail: admin@nrtee-trnee.ca
Web: http://www.nrtee-trnee.ca

# National Round Table Series on Sustainable Development

aussi disponible en français

Canadä

*The National Round Table on the Environment and the Economy is pleased to present this book as a further contribution to the greater understanding of the concept of sustainable development and its practical applications.*

*The views expressed herein are those of the authors and do not necessarily represent those of the National Round Table or its members.*

# Table of Contents

# Preface

## The Journey of a Dream

*"Dreaming is of little value without hard work to fulfill the dream. Hard work is of little value if not driven by a dream."*

The making of this book is the journey of a dream into reality. Many shared this dream, shared the challenges, the hard work in completing this book, and in generating many invaluable by-products along the way.

The journey began with the founding members of the National Round Table on the Environment and the Economy, who recognized that a consensus process could develop the cooperative working relationships and innovative solutions necessary to achieve sustainability. Their experience, and the experience of their counterparts in territories and provinces with round tables, demonstrated the potential of bringing representatives from all sectors of society together to explore and to develop common ground.

A National Task Force on Consensus and Sustainability, co-chaired by Reg Basken and Barry Stuart, was established by the National Round Table to promote, develop and use consensus-based processes in achieving sustainability. The Task Force supported and developed many initiatives which contributed directly or indirectly to the journey leading to this book.

Acknowledging everyone who contributed to the original idea, to developing the "Guiding Principles," and finally to the making of this book would be impossible. May all who participated find appreciation for their contribution in recognizing their energy and insights within the pages of this book.

We thank and acknowledge the founding members of the Round Table who provided initial support for this project: David Johnston, Pierre Marc Johnson, Susan Holtz, Roy Aitken, Jim McNeill, Diane Griffin, David Buzelli, Glen Cummings, Pat Delbridge, Jack McLeod and Leone Pippard.

To George Connell, John Houghton, Tony Hodge, Elizabeth May and other members of the Round Table, we owe special gratitude for sustaining the initial support, and we are grateful for the continued support of the existing Round Table members, notably Dr. Stuart Smith, NRTEE Chair.

For the original members of the Task Force whose work on the Guiding Principles provided the foundation for this book: Reg Basken, Drew Blackwell, Mike Brandt, Charles Brassard, Liza Campbell, Gerry Cormick, D'Arcy Delamere, Lee Doney, Paul Emond, Jane Hawkrigg, Kathryn Heckman, Jerry Hillard, Mike Kelly, Allan Knight, Sheldon McCleod, Carol Reardon, Ruth Schneider, Glenn Sigurdson, Barry Stuart, Joe Weiler, Mark Wedge, Fraser Wilson, Leslie Whitby — and others who joined in along the way — this book is the next stage of their work.

David McGuinty, NRTEE Executive Director and CEO, Gene Nyberg, NRTEE Corporate Secretary and Director of Operations, as well as the staff and former staff at the National Round Table on the Environment and the Economy, and especially those who worked directly with the Task Force, were instrumental in pulling this project together: Anne Dale, Ron Doering, Kelly Hawke-Baxter, Steve Thompson, Allison Webb, and of course, the original catalyst for much of our initial impetus on this journey — Mike Kelly.

The staff and representatives of the territorial and provincial round tables immeasurably helped reach far beyond their respective round tables to include many others within their jurisdictions.

Finally, a very special thanks to Moira Forrest of the NRTEE who had the patience, dedication and, especially important, the consensus skills to bring (push, cajole) the writing team to a final draft.

One or more of the writing team were involved in some of the examples used in this book. None of the examples are used to exemplify a definitive process, but rather to provide practical illustrations that might prompt readers to expand and improve the use of the consensus principles.

New principles may be developed or extracted from these principles, or expressed in a different manner. We lay no claim to have completed the work necessary to exhaustively define the fundamental principles of a consensus process.

However these principles may be expressed, they are all equally vital to the success of a consensus process. Collectively, they weave together the fabric of a consensus process. If one ignores any one of the principles, the process will unravel and the success of the process will be jeopardized. To realize the full potential of a consensus process, all 10 principles must be maintained throughout the entire process.

May everyone find in this book the courage to engage in and design their own consensus process. Further, may the book invite and challenge you to press beyond our work in developing these principles to construct processes that reveal common ground, forge new partnerships, and generate constructive solutions in building and promoting sustainable resolutions of the increasingly complex issues affecting our lives.

# Introduction:

# Consensus Processes, A New Road to Sustainability

T he acceptance of "sustainability" as a practical policy goal and the increasing use of consensus-based processes in the resolution of a broad array of resource management disputes are two important trends of the past decade. This book springs from a marriage of those trends. Experiences in Canada and elsewhere have shown that strategies for achieving sustainability generally need active involvement from, and clear understandings among, a wide array of sectors and groups. This book is a working guide to the use of consensus building in developing the policies and in implementing the programs and projects necessary to achieve a sustainable environment, economy, and society.

Achieving sustainability is not primarily a technical or scientific challenge — although there is much to learn about how ecosystems work and respond to human activity. Nor is the challenge merely to manage our resources more effectively although there is much room for improvement in that, too. Rather, it is about dealing with people and their diverse cultures, interests, visions, priorities, and needs. Unfortunately, the approaches that have been used to manage differences — the courts, the ballot box, and reliance on expertise and authority — are proving insufficient to address the challenge of creating a sustainable society.

As Albert Einstein observed more than half a century ago:

*The world we have created today as a result of our thinking thus far has created problems that cannot be solved by thinking the way we thought when we created them.*

It is through consensus that the "people" differences can be addressed, understood, and resolved within the context of the best technical and scientific information. And it is through building consensus that we develop a collective commitment to manage scarce resources wisely.

In 1991, the Canadian round tables on the environment and the economy launched an intensive effort to understand the nature of negotiation-based processes and their application to issues arising in the pursuit of a sustainable society. Their goal was to identify the essential elements of successful consensus building and, based upon that understanding, establish a set of principles to guide its use.

More than 100 individuals who were members of various round tables participated in the process, which was led by the National Task Force on Consensus and Sustainability. They represented a broad spectrum of Canadians, including representatives of federal, provincial, and municipal governments (both elected representatives and represen-tatives of the public service), First Nation representatives, corporate representatives from natural resource and other sectors, and representatives of a wide range of non-governmental organizations. Every concept and every word in the resulting document, "Building Consensus for a Sustainable Future: Guiding Principles"[1] was subject to intense discussion over a two and one-half year period and was ultimately agreed to by consensus.

This document was formally signed by all provincial and territorial round tables, the National Round Table, and the Canadian Council of Ministers of the Environment. It has since been used as a guide in the development of many contracts and treaties at the local, national, and international levels.

This initial effort and publication generated a broad and favourable response in Canada and abroad. In response to requests for more information on the use of consensus processes, the National Round Table on the Environment and the Economy continued to support a small group drawn from the National Task Force on Consensus and Sustainability. This group was asked to take the work of the

Task Force beyond the development of principles to look at their practical application in addressing real problems.

This book is the result of that request. Written by people with broad experience in using consensus processes, it is addressed to those who might become participants in a process and to those who might manage or mediate a process. Each chapter provides an in-depth discussion of one of the 10 principles and provides practical advice on its application. It outlines typical problems that could arise in applying the principle and gives examples of how those problems can be addressed.

## *What is a consensus process?*

The Canadian round tables agreed on a working definition of a consensus process as it applies to the search for sustainability:[2]

"A consensus process is one in which all those who have a stake in the outcome aim to reach agreement on actions and outcomes that resolve or advance issues related to environmental, social, and economic sustainability.

In a consensus process, participants work together to design a process that maximizes their ability to resolve their differences. Although they may not agree with all aspects of the agreement, consensus is reached if all participants are willing to live with the total package.

....A consensus process provides an opportunity for participants to work together as equals to realize acceptable actions or outcomes without imposing the views or authority of one group over another."

A consensus process can be adapted to fit almost any situation and set of circumstances. It can complement existing governmental and private sector decision-making processes and can be applied within existing mandates and authorities. It does not require special legislation or special mandates. It can result in broadly supported and informed solutions that are practical and feasible and can build the commitments necessary for their implementation.

A consensus process can take many forms. Each situation, with its issues, set of participants, and history prompts the development of a particular configuration and set of specific arrangements within a consensus process. Regardless of the variations, however, consensus processes share one common feature: interaction among participants is face-to-face with the goal of arriving at mutually acceptable outcomes or decisions.

Consensus processes share a number of attributes with other processes that are not consensus-based. For example, citizen participation and public involvement processes also involve diverse interests and parties, often in face-to-face discussions. The essential difference is that these processes are intended to advise decision makers by providing them with a diversity of opinions and advice. In contrast, consensus processes are designed to find the common ground and a mutually acceptable decision that can be implemented or recommended for implementation. The decision makers participate in the process rather than remaining outside and making their decisions independently of the discussions. It is not the involvement of diverse and often differing interests that defines a consensus process. It is their clear and direct role in decision making.

For a consensus process to be an appropriate tool for discovering and implementing a solution, it must be much more than a search for the middle ground. It is the search for common ground that elevates the quality of decisions by bringing to bear the best information and knowledge in a problem-solving atmosphere. Experience has consistently shown that the result will not only enjoy consensus support but achieve innovative, thoughtful solutions that could not be created within the constraints of existing political, legal, or administrative processes.

## Where have consensus processes been used?

In issues arising from the search for sustainability, consensus processes have seen expanding use in Canada and elsewhere during the past three decades. Some examples of their use in Canada include the following:

- Newfoundland — a group of seven partners came together to formulate a program of innovative and sustainable forest management for an area valuable to each in distinct ways.
- Nova Scotia — community stakeholders negotiated a set of principles and criteria for use in finding an appropriate site for a regional solid waste facility.
- New Brunswick — concern over the impact of a pulp mill expansion precipitated a process in which industry, environmental groups, resource organizations, and three levels of government worked together to prepare a consensus document on water quality problems and solutions.
- Prince Edward Island — a debate between recreational users and farmers over use of an abandoned rail corridor was resolved through negotiation.

- Quebec — a government agency set up to conduct public inquiries into environmental issues has increasingly adopted mediation to help parties find their own solutions; mediation was successfully used to settle issues of safety, noise, and heritage value stemming from a highway extension.
- Ontario — mercury contamination of an Aboriginal fishery led to a long-standing dispute concerning health and economic impacts; a negotiated settlement provided financial compensation for the affected First Nations and included provision for a permanent mercury disability fund.
- Saskatchewan — associations representing hunters, trappers, farmers, environmental groups, and tour operators formed a task force and successfully negotiated recommendations aimed at economic diversification based on sustainable wildlife resources.
- Alberta — a large forest company worked with environmental groups, government regulators, Aboriginal peoples, and other resource users to design rules for timber harvesting.
- British Columbia — a plan for a small craft harbour raised environmental concerns regarding impacts on migratory birds; a mediator helped government agencies and parties with environmental and economic concerns to negotiate an acceptable plan for the facility.
- Yukon — after many failed attempts to negotiate a comprehensive land claim, First Nations and the governments of Canada and Yukon used an array of consensus-building techniques and principles to help conclude a treaty. Yukon peace-making circles, built upon consensus principles, promote

sustainable communities by engaging families and communities in developing holistic responses to conflict.
- Canada — the national priority to find common ground on forestry practices and management was addressed by a multistakeholder round table, which negotiated a mutually acceptable set of principles to identify many projects aimed at sustainability for Canada's forests.

These examples — eight of which are described in more detail in Appendix 1 — illustrate the breadth and flexibility possible in the application of consensus processes. Consensus processes can be used in the development of policies, regulations, and procedures, in the design of projects and programs, and in the resolution of issues that arise from their implementation. They can be applied when conflicts are anticipated, when conflicts are emerging, and when conflicts have become crises and positions have hardened.

Throughout the book these and other examples are used to illustrate points and concepts that are set forth. It is emphasized that in the use of such examples we are making no judgements regarding the relative "success" of the processes described. Our only purpose is to illustrate for the reader how the 10 principles set forth can be and have been applied.

## The 10 principles

Consensus building is a powerful and effective decision making and dispute resolution tool. However, like any tool, it must be used with skill for the purposes for which it is intended. Where the process is inappropriately or ineffectively applied, participants could be

## Box I-1

# Building Consensus for a Sustainable Future: 10 Principles

**Principle 1.** **Purpose-Driven**

People need a reason to participate in the process.

**Principle 2.** **Inclusive, Not Exclusive**

All parties with a significant interest in the issues should be involved in the consensus process.

**Principle 3.** **Voluntary Participation**

The parties who are affected or interested participate voluntarily.

**Principle 4.** **Self-Design**

The parties design the consensus process.

**Principle 5.** **Flexibility**

Flexibility should be designed into the process.

**Principle 6.** **Equal Opportunity**

All parties have equal access to relevant information and the opportunity to participate effectively throughout the process.

**Principle 7.** **Respect for Diverse Interests**

Acceptance of the diverse values, interests, and knowledge of the parties involved in the consensus process is essential.

**Principle 8.** **Accountability**

The participants are accountable both to their constituencies and to the process that they have agreed to establish.

**Principle 9.** **Time Limits**

Realistic deadlines are necessary throughout the process.

**Principle 10.** **Implementation**

Commitments to implementation and effective monitoring are essential parts of any agreement.

misled and situations made worse. It was with this in mind that the Canadian round tables developed the 10 principles described in Box I-1 to inform and guide the use of the process.

This book provides the insights and information that will help readers apply these 10 principles effectively in their own situations.

## A step-by-step approach to using a consensus process

The best way to ensure that a consensus process is appropriately and effectively used is to take time to consider whether and how to apply it to a particular situation. The decision to use the process must be a collective one, based upon the informed consent of those who participate in it.

Experience has shown that the consensus-building process usually proceeds through four stages. Often an impartial person who is acceptable to all participants and who is skilled in consensus processes can play an important part in guiding the participants through the process.

### Stage 1. Assessment

The first stage is discussing the process with the potential participants. During this stage the parties begin to identify who might participate, the issues and matters that might be addressed, and whether it is in their interest to participate. The primary objective is to enable potential participants to make an informed decision on whether to participate in a consensus process.

At this point the informed answer might reasonably be: "Maybe — the process is worth exploring, but we need to be certain that the process is fair and the other necessary 'players' will participate in and support the process."

During these assessment discussions it is important to discuss all 10 principles. Principles 1, 2, 3, 8, and 10 are likely to be of particular concern.

### Stage 2. Structuring the process

Participants must design the process (Principle 4), which is usually embodied in a set of written ground rules or protocols formally agreed to by all participants. "Borrowing" a process that was successful elsewhere or engaging an expert to design the process are recipes for disaster: an effective process is one that has been created by and for those who will be using it. Designing and agreeing on the process also gives participants the opportunity to learn to work with one another before beginning discussion of substantive issues.

While all 10 principles will continue to be of interest during the discussion of ground rules, particular attention should be paid to principles 4, 5, 6, and 9.

### Stage 3. Finding the common ground

The search for agreement begins with the commitment to understand, respect, and address one another's concerns and interests (Principle 7). The goal is to reach a joint definition of the issues and, together, to design solutions that work. That is, solutions and agreements must be technically, fiscally, socially, and culturally viable (Principle 10). This search for common ground will be pursued in large sessions, in smaller working groups, and as participants talk about the issues between meetings.

It is important to remember that the search for common ground is different from the identification of middle ground. The best agreements are characterized by innovative solutions and such solutions are possible only where all participants bring to the table their interests, their expertise, and their "rights." Consistently, consensus processes result in agreements that would never be possible under existing decision-making structures.

### Stage 4. Implementing and monitoring agreements

How agreements are reached has much to do with whether and how they are implemented. For example, if agreements are to be implemented, they must be supported by the constituencies as well as by the representatives at the table. This requires an explicit effort by representatives to communicate with constituencies and gain their informed consent during the process (Principle 8).

It is also important that all participants understand from the outset that reaching agreement carries a responsibility to ensure and participate in its implementation (Principle 10). Generally, this requires that, as part of their agreement, the participants define how they will continue to work together in the implementation process. The implementation process should provide mechanisms for dealing with new information and unforeseen problems and for resolving future disputes. Joint monitoring and adaptation should be designed into whatever policy, program, or project is agreed upon.

## Comparing the consensus process with other decision processes

In general, decisions regarding sustainability can be made in two ways: 1) an official decision maker makes the decision or 2) the affected parties make the decision. The first option is the usual way in which such decisions are made. The second describes the consensus process.

### Decision making by "authorities"

This is the conventional means by which environmental decisions are made in Canada.

While many different mechanisms may be used, the underlying model is that one "final" authority — a cabinet minister, an independent review board or panel, a judge, or a host of individual administrators — is empowered to listen to what competing stakeholders have to say, impartially review and weigh their claims and relevant technical information, and then decide. Whatever the specific set of procedures that are used, there tend to be certain characteristics that it is important to identify when comparing these processes to consensus processes:

- those affected or concerned about the issues make their representations to a decision maker,
- there is little or no need or opportunity for those affected to communicate with one another,
- the decision maker is guided by a set of procedures, regulations, and precedents and by advice from various advisers in making the decision,
- the decision is made and announced to those affected, usually with explanations of the reasons for the decision, and
- the competing interests have little or no commitment to the decision that has been made.

### Decision making by consensus

In decision making by consensus there is a fundamental shift in the way in which decisions are made. The various impacted individuals, groups, and organizations — or "stakeholders" — make the decision. One of these stakeholders is likely to be the "authority" who has formal decision-making authority, as discussed above. In this way the formal authority becomes a participant in and supporter of the decision reached by consensus. This ensures that the mandates, policies, regulations, and other concerns of the ministry or other agency are addressed within the consensus decisions. Thus, the participation of such authorities in a consensus process does not "fetter" their authority or abrogate their responsibilities. They choose to enter into a consensus and consensus is reached only if representatives of such authorities are satisfied that their responsibilities are met and that they can recommend the decision for implementation — as they would decisions made under the more usual procedures.

We often say that consensus decisions are reached through "negotiations." Negotiations are a process whereby the participants enter into face-to-face discussions of their views, interests, positions, and preferences for the purpose of finding a mutually acceptable resolution or an "agreement," that is, a "consensus." For example, labour-management negotiations and agreement are a two-party consensus process ending in a consensus. Similarly, participants in consensus processes are often referred to as "negotiators."

Therefore, compared with the more usual decision making by authorities, consensus processes have the following characteristics:
- those directly affected by the decision address their concerns to one another in face-to-face discussions,
- policies, regulations, and precedents are a topic for discussion among the participants,
- the consensus decision is reached by the participants and the reasons for the consensus are clear, and
- all participants are committed to the decision.

As we have discussed, most decisions affecting sustainability in Canada are made by "authorities." The usual opportunity for participation by those affected is through some form of "consultation" process. This "input" into decision making can vary from hearings to workshops to public meetings, with a variety of formats. As the comparison in the accompanying box illustrates, there may be similarities between the consultation and consensus processes, but they are defined by their fundamental difference. Consultation is designed to inform decision makers who will ultimately make the decision. Consensus involves the participants as decision makers.

This creates a very different agenda for stakeholders involved in a consultation process than would be the case in a consensus process. Their overriding goal must be to persuade the relevant authority to make a decision favourable to their own interests. In such a setting, it is not a good strategy to search for the common ground. The more rational strategy is to make the very best case for one's own interests and to cast doubts and aspersions on the arguments and positions of others.

In a consensus process, the participants must address and persuade one another and find solutions acceptable to all. Too often, this distinction between processes is not clear and often overlooked by government. When a consensus process is advocated, the response from authorities may often be: "We're already doing that. We <u>consult</u> with the public all the time."

Both processes should and will continue to be used in Canada. There are many contexts in which a legal requirement or a strong public expectation exists for consultation

**Box I-2**

# Differentiating between "Consultation" and "Consensus"

| Consultation | Consensus |
|---|---|
| **Statement of Purpose** | **Statement of Purpose** |
| "To build consensus as a basis for a decision" | "To build consensus as a basis for a decision" |
| "To inform and become informed" | "To inform and become informed" |
| "To achieve stakeholder input and buy-in" | "To achieve stakeholder input and buy-in" |
| "To meaningfully involve interested parties" | "To meaningfully involve interested parties" |

## The Similarity Ends Here

| Consultation | | Consensus | |
|---|---|---|---|
| **Participants**: | Advocates | **Participants**: | Decision makers |
| **Objectives:** | Hear the voices of many interests | **Objectives:** | Search for a single voice that speaks for all interests |
| **Activity:** | Make representations | **Activity:** | Find trade-offs |
| **Approach:** | Positional | **Approach:** | Interest-based |
| **Process:** | Predetermined by decision maker | **Process:** | Participant-designed |
| **Interaction:** | Contact among parties from none to a lot | **Interaction:** | Relationship builds among the parties through the process |
| **Negotiation:** | Implicit — if at all, in the "back room" and consensus is not required | **Negotiation:** | Explicit — "above board" and includes consultation |
| **Outcomes:** | Many inputs to ultimate decision maker | **Outcomes:** | "One output" — either the actual decision or consensus recommendation to ultimate decision maker |
| **Time lines:** | Prescribed | **Time lines:** | Participant-driven, sometimes within parameters |

**Box I-3**

## Alternative Approaches in Dispute Resolution

*"**Arbitration**"* is an adjudicatory process with an "arbitrator" acting in the capacity of a judge. Disputing interests present their arguments and evidence and the arbitrator "rules," making a decision on behalf of the parties. The parties will be bound by legislative mandate or contractual agreement to accept and adopt the decision of the arbitrator.

*"**Fact finding**"* is similar to arbitration, except that the fact finder's findings are advisory, often in the form of recommendations to some authority and to the parties. The fact-finding process is usually less formal than an arbitration hearing. Fact finding is sometimes referred to as "non-binding" or "advisory" arbitration.

*"**Conciliation**,"* as used in labour relations in Canada, is a hybrid of fact finding and mediation. The conciliator is appointed to write a report on a dispute but seeks to mediate a settlement such that the report reflects the agreement, in all or in part, of the parties. In the United States "conciliation" is often used to describe efforts to resolve disputes without bringing the parties together.

*"**Facilitation**"* refers to the task of managing discussions in a joint session. A facilitator may be used in any number of situations where parties of diverse interests or experience are in discussion, ranging from scientific seminars, to management meetings, to public consultation sessions.

*"**Mediation**"* (as discussed below).

through hearings and public meetings. Also as we shall see in the chapters that follow, the conditions that make possible the use of a consensus process do not always exist (see Chapter 1). Moreover, when a consensus is achieved it may be desirable to hold public meetings or hearings to ensure that the con-sensus reached is broadly acceptable and that no interests or constituencies were ignored.

### The role of the mediator in building consensus

Building consensus among a number of diverse entities with little or no experience in working together, where there is no preexisting structure for discussions, and where the issues are divisive and of deep concern is a daunting challenge. Therefore, it is not surprising that most successful consensus-building efforts in complex disputes over sustainability have been assisted by one or more mediators.

A "mediator" is an independent person, acceptable to all of the participants, whose focus and expertise is in the management and shepherding of consensus processes and in assisting disputing parties to find common agreement. In effect, the mediator is both a "process manager" and a "dispute manager. It is in this context that the term "mediator" is used in this book. The role of the mediator is often confused with that of other third-party or non-involved persons who become involved in the resolution of disputes. Box I-3 defines some of these roles.

To understand the need and role of the mediator it is useful to understand the array of tasks that must be undertaken if the process is to be successful. The Society of Professionals in Dispute Resolution (SPIDR), summarizes the tasks in Appendix 2.

An independent mediator is often best situated to undertake the initial assessment and the development of ground rules. This person can bring experience and expertise to the process. He or she is also able to discuss the process and explore problems in a way that does not compromise the perceived integrity of the process, making it less acceptable to one or more participants. The mediator may also develop and provide training workshops in negotiation and consensus building for the participants.

Formal discussions can usually be made more effective with the help of a mediator. The mediator will help to interpret positions and concerns. He or she will assist the participants, often in separate sessions, in weighing their alternatives. In addition, one or more mediators can be used to arrange and facilitate formal and informal discussions among participants through task groups, subcommittees, and even social settings.

A mediator may carry out a variety of essential process management functions such as preparing agendas, scheduling and keeping participants abreast of meetings, ensuring information is shared, and maintaining meeting notes, summaries, and records, and even drafting language for possible agreements.

## Selecting and managing the mediator

Where a mediator is used, he or she will play a critical role in the process. Therefore, it is important that abilities of the mediator be carefully considered. The list of questions in the accompanying box was suggested in an article in the Canadian Environmental

### Box I-4
## Questions to Ask About Mediators

Does the mediator operate from a base (organization or agency) that is independent of the parties?

Does the mediator have any personal stake (intellectual, economic, or emotional) in the issues?

Does the mediator define his or her expertise in procedural, not technical, terms?

Has the mediator demonstrated that he or she has experience and skill in dealing with complex disputes involving multiple parties; a lack of previous relationships; long-term, possibly irreversible consequences; and differences in technical expertise, level of organization, and personal involvement among the participants?

Have you "checked out" the mediator and/or mediation organization with persons who represent interests and organizations like your own?

Mediation Newsletter.[3] SPIDR has also published an extensive discussion of competencies for mediators, which participants should review before engaging a mediator or entering into a consensus process.[4] While there are a variety of "certifications" that mediators may claim, these may not be based on any broadly recognized and established set of criteria and the participants should satisfy themselves of the mediator's competency and suitability.

A mediator will serve at the pleasure of the parties. That is, if he or she becomes unacceptable to any party, services may be terminated. This apparent "weakness" is, paradoxically, the mediator's greatest asset. It ensures the mediator's independence from any single party and makes the mediator better able to forcefully probe with all parties their concerns, positions, and options.

There are times when different mediators may be used in the different stages of a consensus process. For example, one mediator may be asked to assess and convene a process and another to shepherd the actual discussions. This may arise when a project proponent or ministry asks a mediator to assess with the various stakeholders whether a consensus process would be a viable and acceptable approach to resolving differences. Once the process is convened, the parties may decide to use a different mediator of their own choosing. Indeed, most mediators who have been initially contacted in the manner described above will insist that all of the stakeholders explicitly affirm their desire to continue to use the mediator's services.

Mediators may work individually or in teams. In complex disputes a team of mediators may be able to be more responsive to the time requirements of the parties. There may also be situations where it is possible to hold parallel sessions between task groups or sub-committees on separate issues or topics, further enhancing progress in reaching agreement.

### And, finally...

Participation in a consensus process must not lead to a blind commitment to reach agreement at any cost. It is important to remember that there are situations where, despite their best efforts, the participants are unable to find common ground. In some cases, they may find that they can reach consensus on most issues but agree to disagree on others. Areas of disagreement may then be resolved by a decision maker or an adjudicatory body or upon the development of additional information.

This book is intended to maximize the likelihood that the careful efforts put into developing and pursuing agreements through a consensus process will result in solutions that further progress toward sustainability. Understanding and applying the 10 principles outlined above will help lay a solid foundation for success.

# Chapter 1
# Choosing Consensus Processes

## PRINCIPLE 1: Purpose-Driven

### People need a reason to participate in the process.

"The parties should have a common concern and believe that a consensus process offers the best opportunity for addressing it. This belief requires an informed understanding of consensus processes and a realistic view of available alternatives. If the parties conclude consensus offers a better option to pursue their interest, then a greater commitment to the process and its outcomes will be generated.

Business, government, non-governmental organizations, and other groups can apply consensus processes to a wide range of situations including planning and policy development, regulation, licensing, and site-specific development."

— *Building Consensus for a Sustainable Future: Guiding Principles*

A viable consensus process requires the committed participation of all the stakeholders as they wrestle with technical complexity and value differences. Discussions can be intense and emotions can run high. Representatives and constituents must consider alternative perspectives, ponder unfamiliar facts, and explore innovative solutions. The process is not easy. To meet these exacting demands, all participants must believe that a negotiation-based process should serve their interests.

This chapter highlights the need for a common strength of purpose among participants in a consensus process. It looks at reasons why parties "come to the table" and outlines situations when they should not — not all disputes over the environment and development are right, or ripe, for negotiating.

## What purposes bring parties to a consensus process?

A consensus process must be purpose-driven in that all parties need to see sufficient purpose to participate fully. Their purposes or interests will vary but must be compelling. Several broad motivations turn parties to face-to-face negotiations, for example:

- frustration with the status quo,
- uncertainty about the strength of their position,
- desire for greater and more direct control over the outcome,
- desire to avoid a continuing high profile and politically divisive dispute,
- concern about the costs of a prolonged dispute, and
- desire for finality.

Consensus processes may arise because issues have dragged on for years and frustration drives everyone to look for a way out. For example, the negotiated settlement of a mercury pollution case came about 16 years after the discovery of heavy metal contamination in food fish. During that time, two First Nation communities had been exposed to a serious health risk and had lost guiding and other job opportunities following closure of the recreational fishery. Meanwhile, government agencies had been harshly treated in the press, and the corporate image of companies accused of polluting the waters had been badly damaged. The possibility of more years of the same was disheartening to all.

The mediated settlement of a dispute over siting of a small craft harbour in Sandspit, British Columbia, was also born of prolonged frustration. A federal-provincial agreement had promised a construction start for a harbour by mid-1990. But by late 1991, approvals were still held up due to conflicts over the predicted impact. The possibility loomed of a full environmental assessment panel and two or more years of inquiry, but no harbour. Local politicians turned their frustration into a determined and successful push for mediated negotiation.

Often, parties come to the table because they fear their interests will not be served if a resolution is achieved by other means. Placing an environmental controversy before a board or court often results in an all-or-nothing outcome. For proponents and opponents alike, the risk of defeat may be worse than the unpleasantness of sitting down with an adversary.

Parties may also turn to a consensus process because it offers the best opportunity to influence the substance of the outcome in a major way. Conventional dispute resolution mechanisms generally result in a final decision or compromise by a distant authority with no intimate knowledge of the situation and little stake in the outcome. Such a decision may ignore the essential interests of the parties and overlook opportunities for mutual gains by all parties. In contrast, consensus processes empower the parties to advance interests they understand better than anyone else.

Some parties, particularly government regulatory agencies, may be drawn to consensus processes by the opportunity to defuse a contentious issue that has an embarrassing high profile. The prospect of having disputing parties agree among themselves may be attractive for regulators and politicians who otherwise will have to make a controversial decision. Consensus agreements among chronically disputing parties may also have a stability that is appealing to participants, politicians, and public officials.

Government is not alone in fearing adverse public opinion stemming from long and unpleasant confrontations over the environment. Environmental groups, too, rely heavily on public support and may not want to appear needlessly obstructionist. Participation in a consensus process signals an appealing openness to fair and reasonable solutions. Companies, also, are aware of their public image: consumer support, or boycotts, are increasingly linked to perceptions of corporate citizenship. In one case involving a bitter dispute over a pulp mill, the company (Alberta-Pacific Forest Industries) was drawn to multistakeholder negotiations to develop working relationships with stakeholders, thereby improving its public image.

The financial burden of litigation or hearings is another reason why parties may turn to negotiation. Litigation frequently leaves even parties with very deep pockets wondering whether the whole struggle was worthwhile. It can bankrupt small private or public sector groups. In the mercury pollution case, without government commitment to fund the litigation, neither the bands nor their many members acting as individual litigants could afford a protracted legal battle. The prospect of this expense, combined with the uncertain outcome of litigation, provided a strong inducement for all parties to negotiate.

In many conflicts, parties eventually reach a point where achieving closure on issues becomes a prime motivation. They have better things to do than fight over an issue indefinitely.

Some of these reasons may appear negative: the parties have to be frightened or forced into negotiating. However, as consensus processes become more widely used and their benefits more widely known, more parties will adopt them for the opportunities they offer to

- learn to understand and respect people with different backgrounds and views,
- pool disparate information, thereby fostering better understanding of the many complex technical and scientific issues surrounding environmental controversies,
- invent integrative and adaptive solutions to what seemed to be win/lose situations, and
- rebuild relationships within a community torn by bitter factional conflict.

## When should a consensus process NOT be used?

Not all disputes are appropriate or ready for a consensus approach. Parties need to think about reasons for not going to the table to balance their assessment of the advantages.

One reason for avoiding a consensus process is when one party simply wants to delay matters. While short-term advantages may accrue to a party participating for this reason, that party will ultimately lose credibility when other parties and constituencies come to recognize bad faith involvement. Everyone's interests will be hurt.

The process should also be avoided when a party's sole motivation is to create an appearance of openness. For example, a government agency may attempt to defuse an environmental conflict by creating a committee whose advice will probably be ignored. Using a consensus process for public relations purposes will, in the long run, undermine the credibility of the process and of parties participating for such a reason.

Consensus may also be the wrong route for a party who feels there is a crucial principle at stake over which defeat would be preferable to any appearance of compromise. Underlying this stance may be a well-considered decision that the principle needs to be placed before the courts or legislatures for a formal determination.

A consensus process should also be avoided if any parties believe their interests would be fully satisfied even without negotiations. In this situation, whether the optimism is well founded or not, good faith negotiations are rarely possible. However, it may be useful for parties, perhaps with help from an experienced neutral person, to reexamine the grounds for their confidence before firmly closing the door to consensus negotiations.

Practical limitations can also make it unwise or at least untimely to establish a consensus process. For example, an important party may not be suitably prepared or a community or stakeholder group — particularly a recently formed group — may require more time to

allow representative leadership to emerge. It may be impossible to reach useful agreements without articulate, accountable, and agreed-upon representation. It may also be that constituencies are divided over the question of participating in a consensus process; would-be representatives may wisely decide that the risk of division and resulting loss of support is just too high.

When any of these situations deters important parties from participating, other groups who are more willing and able to negotiate should be very cautious about going ahead with a process. Even if they find apparently good surrogates to represent the missing interest, the end result may well be seen as a sham by both the non-participating groups and the broader public.

An issue may not be right for negotiation at one point in time, but it may become so later. The Alberta-Pacific case well illustrates this dynamic situation. This large forest company asked a professional mediator to investigate whether an emerging controversy over forest management practices might be suitable for consensus building among proponents and opponents. The company felt its best interests lay in negotiation, because although the necessary approvals and permits seemed likely under the existing government, future governments might be more restrictive.

In preliminary meetings the mediator found other stakeholders unwilling to talk. At that time, environmental interests were strongly opposed to the forest management agreement that the provincial government and the company were about to sign. How, they asked, could they sit down to discuss how Alberta-Pacific should manage lands that, in their view, should not be leased to the company without further public discussion? While direct negotiations seemed good in principle, the time was just not right.

Despite the opposition, the government and Alberta-Pacific concluded a forest management agreement. Then questions about how timber would be harvested came to the fore. At that point, the mediator had additional conversations with all stakeholders. Realities had changed. The issue was no longer whether there would be a land allocation to the company, but how stewardship of the leased area could best be achieved. After further reflection and workshops on the principles of consensus building, the major stakeholders decided that their concerns over good management would now be best served by negotiating harvest plans face-to-face.

In summary, parties need to be as open to reasons why they should not negotiate as to reasons why they should. Inappropriate or untimely consensus processes do not leave matters where they were. They can result in more frustration, feelings of betrayal, and worse intergroup relations than before. On the other hand, parties should also realize that time can change the context and make face-to-face meetings worthwhile in the future.

## What are the alternatives to a consensus process?

The opening statement of the principle presented in this chapter required parties to have a realistic view of available alternatives to a consensus process. This is a prerequisite to assessing whether there are compelling advantages for one approach or another.

Canada has great diversity in the forums used for environmental decision making. At every government level, elected bodies, appointed boards and commissions, and a host of individual administrators are empowered to make a wide range of rulings to determine how to use lands and resources or how to manage the impact of one activity on another. Surrounding this decision-making complexity is a wide array of "involvement" mechanisms, ranging from casual and informal consultation, through advisory committees, to formal public inquiries. Courts are also increasingly prominent in the Canadian environmental policy process. In recent years, there have been many highly public cases where political and administrative decisions have come under judicial review.

Despite this diversity, conventional ways of making environmental decisions tend to follow one dominant model:

- The parties who have the most at stake in the issue make their cases to an ultimate decision maker. They do not have much opportunity or need, within the process, to communicate directly with one another.
- The decision maker is supported to varying degrees by competent advisers and will, in making a decision, be guided or even bound by a set of rules and/or precedents. When a decision is reached, it is usually announced with an accompanying explanation of reasons. Appeal processes may be available, but the decision process is the same.

This way of making decisions and accounting for affected interests is, by and large, how the majority of contentious environmental decisions are made in Canada today.

The idea of a dominant model greatly oversimplifies the actual range and specific character of mechanisms. However, it provides a starting point for considering options for resolution and the pros and cons of the consensus approach. In particular it raises the following important issues:

*Issues about relationships with adversaries*

- Do the parties prefer the relative detachment of more formal proceedings?
- Or, do they believe that a future relationship is either necessary or desirable with current adversaries? If so, does consensus offer a better opportunity than conventional approaches to forge such a relationship?

*Issues about the role of stakeholders in framing decisions*

- Do the parties prefer that a wise and dis-interested person or body be the sole arbiter?
- Or, would they feel comfortable crafting the details of their own decision?

*Issues about the role of expert knowledge*

- Do the parties believe that their controversy stems primarily from different interpre-tations of the facts and that the solution lies in getting a highly competent, dispassionate, and expert answer to resolve the issue?
- Or, do the parties consider that the problem is more an inextricable mixture of facts and values demanding direct negotiation among stakeholders, supported as needed by appropriate technical expertise?

*Issues about the importance of rules and precedents*

- Should this dispute be settled on the grounds of either legal precedent or well-established regulations? Does such a framework exist? And, if not, should this specific dispute become a test case to settle issues of general principle or establish broader precedents?
- Or, do the parties see the issues as requiring greater flexibility? Do they want to avoid being bound by past precedents or worrying about the precedent they are setting?
- Do the parties want the benefit of long-established procedural rules such as the right to cross-examine testimony under oath or Robert's rules of order?
- Or, would they prefer to interact more informally and flexibly, observing such rules as they mutually agree are needed?

Each of these issues is enormously difficult and fraught with uncertainty. It may be impossible for parties to settle all procedural questions completely before opting for a consensus process or the dominant model. With a sound knowledge of how environ-mental decisions work without consensus, and by reflecting thoroughly on these critical issues, parties will be better able to decide on the alternatives open to them.

Before leaving the question of alternatives, it is important to make some qualifying remarks. The choices among processes are not always mutually exclusive. For some groups, litigation and/or active protest campaigns, directed at influencing both the public's and politicians' opinions, are essential to gaining a "seat at the table" and being taken seriously by their adversaries during negotiations. Some regulatory review boards are also using consensus processes to help parties agree, or shorten the list of disagreements, before conducting their usual formal reviews. For example, the Bureau d'audiences publiques sur l'environnement (BAPE), a Quebec agency that was originally set up to conduct inquiries into environmental complaints, is increasingly acting as a mediator.

The long series of successful legal battles that First Nations have fought over the past decade has unquestionably influenced the willingness of other parties to negotiate over land and resource issues. Environmental groups have relied extensively on direct action and the threat or reality of litigation. What this means is that the consensus process should be seen not as a wholly separate approach but, in many cases, as complementary to and even dependent on more confrontational options.

## What should parties ask before committing to a consensus process?

Potential participants in a consensus process may be hesitant to commit to a process. Sometimes they are unsure whether their interests are best served by participating. Often their reluctance stems from inadequate understanding of the process. However, if such parties are willing to learn about the process and assess its usefulness in terms of their interests, they can often clarify what they really want and need.

The following questions can help parties decide whether they have sufficient purpose to join in a consensus process:
- What is it that our organization really wants and values?
- What would we need to get and how would this dispute have to end for our interests to be met?
- What is likely to happen if we do not go to the bargaining table? Worst case? Best case? Most probable?
- What is the best alternative strategy we could pursue if there are no negotiations or a consensus settlement?[5]
- How might our opponent(s) answer the above questions?

These overlapping questions all relate to whether there is a sufficient and informed sense of purpose among the parties. To

coordinate a thorough assessment on "whether to talk" often requires the help of a neutral "convenor." In the Alberta-Pacific case, a professional mediator with wide experience in negotiations conducted a detailed assessment — including workshops on the use of the consensus process for stakeholder groups. His work enabled parties to make an informed choice on whether, how, and when to proceed.

## How can parties maintain a sense of purpose throughout the process?

Keeping parties at the negotiating table is not always easy. Much can change as a consensus process unfolds. For one thing, the powerful emotions that energized parties at the start may dissipate once discussions are under way and some preliminary progress is made. This is particularly likely among parties who see the consensus process as a way to defuse a politically dangerous situation. The resulting complacency is understandable but risky — care must be taken to ensure that the level of commitment is maintained for the difficult work that lies ahead.

There is also an ever-present danger that one or more of the parties will become dis-enchanted with the conduct or progress of the process but not wish to protest formally or withdraw for fear of seeming unreasonable or uncommitted.

Their dissatisfaction will show up in lack of attention and attendance and in decreased commitment to search for the common ground. This situation is most likely to arise in a complex process that requires substantial time for the discussions.

External events may also alter the parties' willingness to negotiate. This may present no problems, as when, in the course of joint problem solving, a party sees that its primary concerns are no longer at stake and withdraws from the process.

For the most part, however, consensus processes do not easily withstand a decrease in group energy and commitment. How, then, can this be avoided? First and perhaps most important is for the process to yield results. If negotiations are progressing, each party's stake in the process grows steadily. Too much good work would be wasted if momentum were allowed to dwindle.

The benefits of a better working relationship, the resolution of technical complexities, the discovery of integrative solutions that make everyone better off, and the approaching prospect of a durable settlement are all new and powerful attractions. These can replace the more negative motivations of fear and frustration that got the parties started.

Given the importance of shared accomplishments for maintaining a sense of purpose, the challenge then is to mark progress. Early negotiation and agreement on process ground rules can be doubly beneficial: it gives parties a first opportunity to work together successfully, helping them develop a taste for collaborative problem solving. And it enables them to set interim check points during which they will assess progress and decide whether to recommit to the process.

A check point may be related to some specific accomplishment. In the Alberta-Pacific negotiations, an initial agreement on draft timber harvest guidelines provided such a milestone. The initial ground rules for these negotiations set a deadline for agreement on this interim product at about 90 days from the beginning of substantive discussions. Several of the participants had entered the process with

commitment but also considerable doubts as to whether any common ground would be discovered. They needed to see tangible results within a reasonable period. Although final agreement on the timber harvest guidelines took longer than expected, a working draft was produced by the target date, giving everyone enough encouragement to carry on.

The role of time limits is further discussed in Chapter 9. The relevant point here is that milestones and deadlines focus and energize the parties, giving them continuous positive feedback that the process is working. This is essential to maintaining the sense of purpose required for reaching and implementing a consensus agreement.

## Conclusion

Consensus processes are gaining wide interest among parties who have become disillusioned with conventional means for participation in environmental decision making. For many caught up in a bitter and protracted controversy, face-to-face negotiations may seem the only way out. Before committing to join a consensus process, however, all parties need to think through the issues that have been presented in this chapter. With or without the help of an experienced professional, they should reflect on how consensus — and alternative routes — could further their purposes. As far as possible they should carefully consider the same for their adversaries.

In many cases the conclusion will be that consensus building offers the best prospect for better decisions for all. The basic message of this chapter is that purposes must be examined, alternatives considered, and the pros and cons of involvement in a consensus approach most carefully analysed.

# Chapter 2
# Making Consensus Processes Inclusive

## PRINCIPLE 2: Inclusive, Not Exclusive

**All parties with a significant interest in the issues should be involved in the consensus process.**

"Care needs to be taken to identify and involve all parties with a significant interest in the outcome. This includes those parties affected by any agreement that may be reached, parties needed to successfully implement it, or who could undermine it if not included in the process.

It is sometimes appropriate for those representing similar interests to form a caucus or coalition.

When decisions require government action, the appropriate authorities should participate.

The integrity of a consensus process may be compromised if the parties are not given the opportunity to determine their representatives through their own processes and mechanisms, particularly in circumstances where the direct interests of the parties will be affected by the outcome."

— *Building Consensus for a Sustainable Future: Guiding Principles*

Disputes over sustainability — over the environmental, social, cultural, and economic merits of projects and policies — can deeply affect the interests of many diverse stakeholders (see Box 2-1). A principal advantage of consensus processes compared with judicial or administrative forums lies in the expanded opportunity they provide for direct participation by affected interests.

Yet, as the circle of participation widens, many difficulties must be overcome — logistical problems and concerns over the legitimacy, cost, and effectiveness of multiparty negotiations. This chapter addresses the reasons for being inclusive rather than exclusive, describes the challenges in adhering to this principle, and suggests ways to enable the participation of all parties with a significant stake in the outcome of a consensus process.

The chapter is structured around the following questions:

- Why should consensus processes be inclusive, not exclusive?
- What arguments are raised against being "maximally inclusive," and how are these countered?
- Who should be at the table? What criteria apply in determining whether there is a good reason, a "significant interest," that makes a party's participation vital?
- What can be done to ensure all relevant parties are identified?
- How can large numbers of stakeholders be accommodated?

Before pursuing these questions, it is important to note that sitting at the consensus table is not the only way for interested parties to be involved. Ideally, the most important stakeholders will be there. But some parties may not want direct involvement. They may feel other groups adequately represent their interests; they may only be affected by a small aspect of the overall issue being addressed; they may not care enough to invest the time that involvement requires; or they may be reluctant to participate because of their future role in a regulatory decision about the consensus recommendation. Nevertheless, an effective process can develop appropriate access and involvement for all parties. There can be different "circles" of participation in and around a consensus process.

It is especially important for those directly involved in negotiations to keep those with a direct stake or an implementation role well informed of the building blocks of the final agreement. With the approval of all parties at the table, a mediator can brief groups who are not at the table, reducing the risk of unpleasant surprises.

In the mediated negotiation over harbour development at Sandspit, British Columbia, the organization representing the Haida Nation felt it had no direct stake in the deliberations over facility siting. Organization members chose not to take part in the discussions but were kept informed on an ongoing basis. In this way, they kept abreast of discussions and could be sure no outcomes were taking shape that could affect their interests.

Stakeholders who are marginally affected may not wish to follow the progress of consensus building closely. They can be generally informed by the media and given opportunities for direct input through special sessions and participation in subcommittees or public meetings. In the Sandspit harbour case, information columns were placed in local newspapers. These contained questions frequently asked by the public and replies drafted by

**Box 2-1**

# The Typical "Cast" and Their Significant Interests in Sustainability Issues

Each consensus process has its own special "cast" and issues. The following list illustrates typical categories of parties and some significant interests such parties tend to emphasize:

## Category

## Significant Interest (illustrative)

| Category | Significant Interest (illustrative) |
|---|---|
| Proponents: private or public sector | Advancing the project<br>Minimizing major public opposition |
| Regulators: federal, provincial, and municipal government agencies with formal rules and responsibilities applicable to the issue | Maintaining consistent environmental standards as required by law/regulation<br>Protecting and enhancing access to harvestable resources (e.g., wildlife, sport fish, etc.)<br>Maintaining public confidence in the agency and the government |
| First Nations and other Aboriginal groups | Exercising stewardship and use rights<br>Improving social and economic conditions of Aboriginal communities |
| Environmental groups | Protecting sensitive species and places<br>Maintaining nature's ability to sustain and regenerate itself |
| Other miscellaneous non-governmental organizations such as resource user groups and neighbourhood associations | Protecting wildlife resources<br>Preventing negative socio-economic impacts of development |
| Municipal councils | Promoting local economic development<br>Maintaining good relations among diverse constituents |
| Organized labour | Protecting/increasing employment<br>Workplace safety<br>Various other social concerns (with much variation among unions) |
| Local business | Protecting/enhancing local business opportunities<br>Local economic development |

subcommittees of the negotiating group. Information meetings were held regularly, while more formal "open houses" were used when a tentative consensus had been reached. Creating opportunities for inclusion tailored to the needs of all circles of interest improves the likelihood of innovative and viable agreements and broadens public support for them.

## Why be inclusive?

Three strong arguments exist for making consensus processes as inclusive as possible. First, inclusiveness lends credibility to the process: historically underrepresented groups have worked hard in the last few decades to gain "standing" in environmental decisions; they would not accept a return to more exclusive processes. Second, inclusiveness ensures that the interests and insights of all significantly affected parties are brought to bear on the problem. Finally, inclusiveness invites cooperation and understanding from parties who can "make or break" the implementation of an agreement. These arguments are examined briefly below.

### Process credibility

Demands for more direct and influential public involvement in environmental decision making have been heeded only in the past two or three decades. Significant recognition of Aboriginal peoples' rights in relation to lands and resources is even more recent. Today, it is inconceivable that any major development with potential environmental effects could proceed without some involvement by parties who could be affected. Any new approach to environmental decision making will lose credibility and public acceptance if it appears to be closing the doors to wide-ranging participation.

### Encompassing all concerns

Broadening the scope of effective participation significantly enhances the quality, creativity, and acceptance of the process and outcome. The greater the diversity of perspectives, experience, and knowledge within problem-solving teams, the less the chance that important information will be overlooked and the better the chance of finding innovative solutions to seemingly intractable problems.

In the Sandspit negotiations, participants gradually became aware of the complementary roles of scientific and everyday "folk" knowledge. To questions about the ecology of local waterfowl species, biologists could apply their expertise in population dynamics and natural history; local people, on the other hand, could provide information based on much longer-term, if less rigorous, observations of these species. Integrating these perspectives enabled the mediation team to develop a richer and more sophisticated understanding of the local ecology.

### Implementing agreements

The third argument for inclusiveness is pragmatic: turning consensus into action can be a complex and challenging endeavour (see Chapter 10). It depends on the understanding and support of everyone involved in imple mentation, including parties with regulatory responsibilities and necessary funding authorities. Excluded parties sometimes make a special effort to oppose someone else's consensus decision. Including such parties in a timely and effective manner can prevent unnecessary opposition and foster a broadly based sense of ownership among all affected parties.

## Why NOT be inclusive?

Resistance to inclusion has three basic reasons. One centres on managing the difficult logistics of a process with large numbers of participants. Another stems from concern that some participants have no interest in reaching consensus and will stymie the efforts of other parties. Finally, opposition arises from the belief that broadly inclusive consensus processes usurp the legitimate and traditional role of elected governments and their officials.

### Inclusion is impossible for logistical reasons

The objection to maximum inclusion on logistical grounds usually stems from the assumption that large groups are inherently unwieldy. How can everybody be seated at the bargaining table and still have any chance of successfully communicating, let alone reaching consensus?

Excluding directly affected interests can and has produced greater barriers to agreement than managing the difficulties of including many parties. To exercise such exclusion is to lose sight of the very purpose of consensus. It is quite probable that excluded parties will find another way to convey their concerns, and this may undermine the work already done to reach consensus in a smaller and exclusive circle. While large numbers pose real logistical problems, these are not insurmountable, as shown later in this chapter.

### Inclusion would kill the consensus process

The idea that some parties simply have no interest in reaching consensus is often put forward to deny their participation. There are often pressures to exclude people who seem uncooperative or unwilling to budge from strident initial positions. There are also pressures to exclude parties who lack any incentive for reaching a timely settlement, who prefer the status quo, or who seek highly visible battles in the press or courts to secure wider public support.

Whatever the reason for uncooperative participation, those determined to reach a swift consensus are strongly tempted to leave such parties out. This is almost always a mistake since such parties can later undermine any negotiated settlement. General experience in consensus processes reveals that "difficult" people often act as they do because their concerns have not been acknowledged or respected. Given the chance to participate in a forum that legitimizes their concerns, many people become more cooperative.

Problems posed by those whose interests are not served by reaching consensus are best confronted at the beginning of negotiations. At this time, all parties should be asked whether they genuinely seek a settlement, and their commitment to the goal of consensus should be written into the ground rules. Attempting to secure commitments at the outset helps identify any party whose interests are not served by a timely consensus. The object is not to prejudge and exclude such groups but rather to invite their involvement in assessing how their interests can be served through participation. If, after these deliberations, key parties choose not to participate, others may see no use in proceeding or, alternatively, may go ahead with the consensus process but find other ways to keep non-participants informed.

### Inclusion is undemocratic

A frequently voiced argument against highly inclusive consensus processes stems from the idea that ad hoc decision groups are contrary to fundamental tenets of democracy. This objection often emerges over the use of an interest-based consensus process for policy issues: "Didn't we elect town councils, provincial legislatures, and federal members of Parliament precisely so that accountable representatives could resolve public questions? Does it not undermine that system to allow a hodge-podge of non-governmental organizations, regulators, developers, and the like to reach binding agreements on critical and difficult public issues that affect the 'general interest'?" Chapter 8 examines the challenge of ensuring accountability. The following paragraphs briefly outline responses to the suggestion that a consensus process subverts the democratic process.

At all levels of government in Canada, elected politicians delegate much of the day-to-day responsibility for environmental management to non-elected officials. For example, in practice, it would only be in highly exceptional circumstances that the minister of fisheries and oceans would personally review the details of area fishing plans: this responsibility is typically delegated through the deputy-ministerial and director levels to regional or field offices. There, appointed officials make the decisions that powerfully affect the livelihoods of fishers and their communities. Recently, some groups have successfully pressed for consensus forums and co-management of the resources to replace dependence on the discretion of departmental employees.[6] To suggest that a consensus process usurps what would otherwise be the thoughtful direct involvement of the elected official ignores the nature of bureaucratic decision making in Canada today. The move toward consensus processes involving non-government groups as well as government agencies broadens the process in a way that

reinforces the participatory foundation of a democracy.

This critique of consensus processes is misguided in other ways. No consensus process used in Canada to date has been advocated as an alternative to the exercise of legitimate government mandates. The consensus building initiated through the use of mediated negotiations in federal environmental assessment reviews serves as an alternative to appointed advisory panels. These initiatives no more deny final ministerial responsibility for project approval than do appointed advisory panels. Box 2-2 illustrates how the parties in one process clarified the protection of their rights and mandates, as they participated in consensus building.

The importance of direct government participation, especially by agencies with regulatory duties, was noted earlier. Their presence within a multiparty group operating by consensus means no decision will be allowed to violate any legally required mandates. For example, in the Sandspit harbour negotiations, the federal Department of Fisheries and Oceans Habitat Management Division was directly represented on the negotiating team. Official habitat policy was not negotiable. This meant that although there was flexibility in the siting and development of the proposed harbour, the Department required habitat "compensation" consistent with established standards.

Ensuring direct involvement of a public agency is an effective way to avoid encroaching on ministerial responsibilities and political accountability. It ensures public agencies' formal responsibilities and requirements are built into the consensus decision. Constructing a consensus process that leaves final approval to elected representatives incorporates political accountability while advancing participatory democracy.

## *Who should be at the table?*

Anyone who could be significantly affected by the decision should be included at the table. For environmental projects, stakeholders include the proponents — the intended beneficiaries — and those in geographic proximity who may be affected by spill-over effects; new developments may bring more people and changes in the landscape as well as threats to environmental quality, human health, safety, and privacy. These parties are essential both to ensure the fairness of a process and because they best represent their

---

**Box 2-2**

# Ground Rules for Clarifying Rights and Responsibilities

A.  The intent of this process is to provide the opportunity for all parties with a stake in the outcome to participate in a voluntary process to deal with issues and resolve disputes so that, whenever possible, final decisions are made on the basis of recommendations supported by a consensus as opposed to being unilaterally imposed. Decisions in the dispute resolution process shall be by consensus. Consensus shall mean the "general agreement of all participants on a package of decisions or recommendations" and shall embody the following concepts:

1.  Consensus does not mean total concurrence on every aspect of a decision, but all participants must be willing to accept the overall decision package.

2.  If a participant withholds agreement on an issue, that participant is responsible for explaining how its interests are adversely affected or how the proposed agreement fails to meet its interests. The participant withholding agreement must propose alternatives, and other participants must consider how all interests may be met.

3.  When initial agreement is achieved, some participants may need to take the agreement back to their constituencies or a higher decision-making authority for ratification.

4.  Once consensus is reached on the overall package, it is assumed to be binding.

B.  All participants to a recommendation on which consensus has been achieved agree to exercise their rights, mandates, and responsibilities consistent with the recommendation and to take such further steps as may be necessary to give it effect.

C.  If no consensus is achieved through this process, each participant will exercise its rights, responsibilities, and mandates as it sees fit — unfettered as to its statutory decision-making responsibilities and without prejudice to its rights and obligations by reason of having participated in the process.

*— The Northeast B.C. "2005" Initiative*

own interests and concerns. The parties most affected are often in a much better position to talk sensitively of trade-offs than, for example, regulatory agencies that neither know the local context nor have to live with the final decision.

In determining who should be at the table, the parties must consider who will play an important role in implementing whatever consensus is reached. All too often, public policies are decided with little input from mid-level or field staff who will have to put the agreement into practice. Those responsible for implementation can provide a sobering reality check for consensus-building teams who propose idealistic but impractical solutions. In planning for the Sandspit harbour, the federal Department of Public Works and consulting marine engineers provided essential guidance on alternative sites and designs. Options that seemed sensible to community representatives and environmental groups were, in some cases, technologically unfeasible. Readily available explanations saved the mediation team from time-consuming pursuit of impractical solutions.

A third guideline for inclusion suggests involving anyone with the power or motivation to undermine a negotiated outcome. Initial participants in a consensus process are often reluctant to open the door to those known to have taken hard-line positions on the issues. But such positions are not likely to soften if these parties are excluded. Indeed, the opposite can be true. Enabling influential groups to participate from the outset offers the best insurance against having to deal with their opposition to a consensus reached without them.

It is extremely difficult to ensure the involvement of widely dispersed interests who stand to benefit from a proposed development. For example, in the case of a proposed solid waste disposal site, thousands of households may be relying on timely siting and development. Yet these people may face more difficulty organizing their involvement in a deliberative process than would a much smaller number of people who live near a proposed site and are vigorously opposed to it.

Other interests are even harder to involve and represent, for example, future generations affected by projects with long-term effects (e.g., clear cutting or radioactive waste storage) or, indeed, the non-human interests in whose name many environmental battles are fought. The existence of hard-to-define and hard-to-represent interests remains one of the biggest challenges in public decision making. By explicitly asking the question "who should be represented here?" consensus processes offer a better opportunity than more formal settings to address this challenge.

### What can be done to identify all relevant parties?

One of the first tasks of a new consensus group is to look around and ask, "Who is not here who should be?" It can be a difficult question to raise simply because it has usually been extraordinarily difficult to assemble those already at the table. Typically, old and often bitter adversaries are sitting across from each other for the first time. To open the issue of additional participants seems to be asking for trouble. Yet, the issue must be addressed. In this preliminary stage, a mediator can play an important role, urging group members to be open-minded as they explore who else has a stake and whose presence might provide a hitherto-neglected dimension in finding solutions.

In the Alberta-Pacific case, the mediator conducted an extensive round of interviews with the many clearly identified parties. He asked each one who else was needed, was affected, or had the power to derail any agreement reached. In this way an ever-widening circle was identified and steps were taken to involve each party in some way.

In addition to brainstorming and individual networking, public communications are essential for discovering additional participants. Articles or advertisements in the media reduce the possibility that some group may not hear about the process. In the Sandspit harbour case, well-advertised public discussions were held to let people know mediated negotiations were getting under way. The resulting publicity alerted several previously uninvolved organizations and at least one of these sought a seat at the table. Subsequently, when the consensus group decided more explicit public notification was needed, they inserted a list of representatives and a contact person in the local newspaper to encourage other potential participants to come forward. When critics of the consensus recommendations questioned the representativeness of the process, the consensus group could point to these early and well-publicized opportunities for expanding participation.

Parties in a consensus process should anticipate the emergence of new parties as options for resolution become better defined. Developments during the process may cause some movement from the outer to the inner circle of participation. Framing ground rules at the outset of the process on how to "seat" latecomers will better prepare the original

parties for such contingencies. In the Western Newfoundland model forest process, initial members of the consensus group anticipated the emergence of additional parties and framed a detailed ground rule on expanding its membership (Box 2-3 provides examples of the membership ground rules used in this and several other mediation processes).

## How can large numbers of stakeholders be accommodated?

It is widely assumed that only small problem-solving groups can be effective. As group size increases, difficulties multiply in communicating, arranging logistics, and reaching unanimous agreement. Experience shows this need not be an insurmountable problem.

Many groups that are initially interested in participating may subsequently decide their interests are not really at stake or are already well represented by others. In the Sandspit case, a local planning group applied for membership on the mediation team, in part because a similar group was already represented. After discussion with the mediator and other Sandspit representatives, the group concluded that its interest, the timely completion of the development, was already well represented. This underscores an important point: inclusive representation does not mean every party must be at the table, but that all significant interests should be represented there.

Where many groups and organizations have an interest in the negotiations, one effective solution can be to form caucuses: groupings of groups whose interests are similar enough that they can work together. Even if all caucus members attend plenary sessions on behalf of their individual constituencies, caucuses

## Box 2-3

# Sample Ground Rules for Expanding Group Membership

### Western Newfoundland Model Forest Process

1. The Management Group can at any time be expanded with the consent of "consensus members."

2. The Management Group shall have regard to such considerations as the following in determining whether to expand its membership:

    i) the nature of the Interest represented by the proposed expansion of membership;

    ii) whether the Interest is:

    a) represented through a current member;

    b) meaningfully represented otherwise; or

    c) might be meaningfully represented through some other involvement whether as an Observer, representation on a Working Group, a participant in a Workshop, or otherwise;

    iii) whether a prospective individual or group has come forward who is willing to represent the Interest and who has the desire and commitment and could make a meaningful contribution to the MFP;

    iv) striving to maintain a balance among representatives of interests, and between representation and effectiveness.

An "Open Seat" will be continuously maintained throughout the MFP to signal the commitment of the management group to expand its membership having regard to these considerations and to generally conduct its affairs and undertake activities "openly" with full opportunity for meaningful involvement. — Ground Rules

### Alberta-Pacific Forest Management Task Force

Additional interest or stakeholder groups may be invited to participate by concurrence of the Task Force. — Task Force Procedures

### Sandspit Small Craft Harbour Mediation Process

The participation of any additional parties will require the review and approval of the Principal Participants. In making this review the Principal Participants shall consult with the Mediator. — Ground Rules

### Saskatchewan Wildlife Diversification Task Force

In circumstances where additional members that the WD believes should participate in these activities [are] identified, or a group comes forward indicating its wish to do so, any such group may become a member, and any changes to these operating rules that might be suggested at that time, only with the consensus of the WD Task Force. — *Operating Rules* reduce the number of concerns introduced and simplify consensus building. They also provide opportunities for information sharing and problem solving among groups of similar interests. Caucusing was used extensively in the Alberta-Pacific Forest Management Task Force.

Delegating tasks to subcommittees or working groups is another useful way to deal with large numbers of stakeholders. Assignments that would be difficult to complete in rooms of 30 or 40 people can be tackled in subgroups representing those with a major interest in the specific topic. In the Sandspit case, subcommittees were used to generate options for dealing with the most complex questions. Once a subcommittee agreed on its draft, the text went back to the full team for discussion, review, and adoption. In the Alberta-Pacific case, a committee representing all the caucuses developed the first draft of an overall set of forestry operating guidelines.

Working groups can also be used to extend participation to parties that are not at the main table but who have expertise or interest in a particular topic. Membership on a working group enables such a party to contribute to the overall consensus in a way that reflects its stake in the outcome.

It should be reiterated that by establishing reliable means for informing those not at the table — the parties in the outer circles of participation — a consensus team can reduce the demand for direct participation by many other groups and interests.

# Conclusion

Until recently, difficult decisions balancing the interests of many stakeholders affected by development or resource policies were made within narrow administrative or judicial forums. Those were simpler times and, in the short run, it is still easier for a few parties to get together and reach agreement on such matters. However, the doors of participation have opened and experience demonstrates the advantages of all key stakeholders working together — greater creativity, fairness, credibility, and social acceptance. The benefits of inclusionary decision making in comparison with the exclusionary decision making of the recent past are becoming much clearer. Many of the most serious environmental problems that Canadians still face reflect an era when the full range of interests was inadequately addressed.

The inclusion of a far broader circle, made up of those who propose, regulate, oppose, or just wish to reflect critically and influentially on the consequences of development, is the emerging alternative. Consensus processes offer the best opportunity for reaping the benefits of greater inclusion on sustainability issues. A fully inclusive process is beneficial, challenging, and achievable.

# Chapter 3
# Voluntary Participation in Consensus Processes

## PRINCIPLE 3: Voluntary Participation

### The parties who are affected or interested participate voluntarily.

"The strength of a consensus process flows from its voluntary nature. All parties must be supportive of the process and willing to invest the time necessary to make it work. The possible departure of any key participant presses all parties to ensure that the process fairly incorporates all interests.

A consensus process may complement other processes. It asks the parties to make their best efforts to address issues through consensus. If that process fails, participants are free to pursue other avenues."

— *Building Consensus for a Sustainable Future: Guiding Principles*

Consensus means having all parties say yes; but yes is not meaningful unless they could have said no. The ultimate right to say yes or no is what gives significance to the accomplishment of consensus.

The freedom to participate is at issue when a consensus group is being established and through the entire process. This chapter examines the significance of voluntary participation, asking:

- How does a voluntary process help parties decide whether to come to the table?
- How can parties design the process to ensure voluntary participation?
- How does a voluntary process lead to more constructive negotiations?
- How does a voluntary process make implementation of the consensus more likely?

### How does a voluntary process help parties come to the table?

The first step in getting parties to engage in a consensus process is difficult and fragile. The challenge is to enable parties to explore whether their interests could be served through negotiations without threatening those interests. To assess the potential advantages and disadvantages of participating in negotiations, parties need a good understanding of what it would be like to work with rather than against other parties. However, they will be reluctant to begin preliminary discussions if they risk being locked into a high-risk process. What must be made clear at the outset is that parties have the right to leave at any time — the right to leave is what makes it safe to come in.

In practical terms, one way of convening a potential consensus process is to invite parties to an exploratory meeting, without any obligation to participate in further sessions. This helps overcome parties' understandable reluctance to sit down with long-time adversaries. Representatives can credibly explain to their constituencies that no risk is involved: "We'll talk to them about the pros and cons of further meetings but stay free to say 'thanks, but no thanks'."

Considering what is at stake in joining a consensus process, this freedom is of clear significance. Temporarily, a consensus process does level the playing field, suspending power imbalances for as long as the process continues (see discussion in Chapter 6). However, power is neither eliminated nor neutralized, it simply gets "parked" outside — both sides in a dispute may feel negotiations will mean compromise of certain advantages, interests, and even fundamental values. For example, project proponents with deep pockets and strong legal precedents may feel they will lose their advantage by sitting down with local opponents. Conversely, a local group opposed to a proposed development may fear that negotiations will lose them popular support and any high moral plane they may have achieved. In the midst of these fears, freedom to walk away from the process is crucial. Nothing but an evening can be lost by talking about whether to go on talking.

In decisions over the environment and development in Canada, consensus building is the newcomer. Potential participants are usually well aware that more conventional if adversarial options are open to them by custom or even legal right. The voluntary nature of participation prevents the possible perception among stakeholders that such rights are being violated. It must be made very clear to parties that should they decide not to participate or if consensus fails, they will not have lost or diminished their ability to pursue their interests through other more conventional means.

## How can parties design the process to ensure voluntary participation?

Parties in a consensus process have one very significant opportunity to maximize everyone's freedom of choice. This arises when they design their own process. The broader aspects of process design are discussed in Chapter 4. Here the focus is on how ground rules, established at the outset, can ensure that participation is voluntary while increasing the likelihood that parties will choose to participate.

Several items generally included in ground rules are especially significant. First and perhaps most important is the way parties define consensus and set out what happens if consensus is not reached. Some groups claim to operate by "virtual consensus" or "consensus minus one." Unfortunately, this use of consensus is often taken to mean agreement that is not necessarily unanimous[7] — a definition that invites major problems. For example, such approximate consensus allows majority parties to gang up against the minority interests, injecting threats and blame into a process that is supposed to build working relations. No minority interests will want to participate if that kind of conduct is allowed. As parties develop their ground rules, they need to define very clearly what they mean by consensus. Various definitions of the term used in several cases appear in Box 3-1. While there is room for different wording, it is essential that unanimity be explicitly and exclusively the rule.

Along with a strict definition of consensus, the ground rules can also include rules that prescribe what happens in the event of a stalemate. To address the concern that a rule of unanimity dooms the process to impasse and hasty exits, parties can outline a sequence of steps to take when the going gets rough.

To reduce the possibility of prolonged stalemate, parties may wish to define a specific dispute resolution mechanism in the ground rules. For example, they can engage a mediator when unassisted communication breaks down. In some cases it may be possible for parties to include others at a more senior organizational level in discussions on "stalemated" issues.

To address an impasse over complicated technical issues, the ground rules may call for the assistance of experts to review the facts. Experts can be chosen by common agreement of the parties or by setting up a panel for which each side in the dispute chooses a member. Parties can decide in advance to accept whatever interpretation their experts can agree on.

Ground rules may also outline measures to take if a participant decides to withdraw from the process. Withdrawal need not be a death-blow for the process. Instead, by design, it can trigger actions that make recovery possible. Parties can agree in advance that if they become so disenchanted as to consider withdrawal, they will give other participants sufficient prior notice and the opportunity to talk about reasons for withdrawal before making a final decision. This measure discourages idle threats of withdrawal and, by allowing for a cooling-off period, reduces the likelihood of impulsive exits. It also ensures the rest of the group will have to listen carefully to arguments that the process is not meeting the needs of disaffected parties. The following guideline was adopted in

**Box 3-1**

# Some Definitions of Consensus Used in Canadian Processes

## Alberta-Pacific Forest Management Task Force

    A. Defining Agreement

        1. Agreement is defined as the explicit concurrence of the caucuses represented on the Task Force. While there will be no voting and, therefore, a quorum is not relevant, explicit concurrence requires that all caucuses be represented.

        2. Interim understandings reached during the discussions of the Task Force are tentative pending agreement on a total package addressing the issues before the Task Force, unless otherwise agreed.

        3. The Task Force may agree to a package that includes all but a few specified provisions. Should this occur, the participants will mutually define areas of disagreement and agree upon how the remaining issues will be addressed.

In no case will there be a statement of what portion of the caucuses were in favour of or opposed to any provision on which there is remaining disagreement.

— Task Force Procedures

## Sandspit Small Craft Harbour Mediation Process

The Parties agree to operate by consensus which shall mean the agreement of all the principal participants. — Ground Rules

## Western Newfoundland Model Forest Process

*Consensus: the explicit concurrence of all members as represented by the "consensus members" ... Explicit concurrence requires that all members are represented in arriving at the consensus. — Ground Rules*

the Western Newfoundland model forest process for situations where one party disagrees with a pending decision:

*If one or a few Members disagree with a proposed decision, then that Member is responsible for demonstrating clearly that the item at issue is a matter of such principle that he or she cannot accept the decision. Or, the Member must clearly show why and how he or she would be specifically and differentially impacted by the proposed decision.*

*If the dissenting Member can demonstrate either condition, then it becomes incumbent upon the rest of the Members to make an explicit effort to address those concerns. —* Western Newfoundland model forest process — Ground Rules

By establishing reciprocal responsibilities to address deal-breaking differences, this kind of rule makes justifiable departure a valid option while discouraging spurious threats of withdrawal. And in the event of an impasse, the ground rules of the Western Newfoundland model forest process provide an example of a possible approach to resolving an impasse:

> *In the event that an impasse develops, an appropriate conflict resolution process will be agreed upon and adhered to by the Members. Some possible steps in the process may include, but is [sic] not limited to, the following measures:*
>
> i) *involvement of the Board of Directors in the discussions to assist in the further exploration of the issue(s);*
> ii) *involvement of mediation assistance, including the possibility of engaging a professional mediator to assist the Management Group in reaching a solution of the issue(s) dividing them;*
> iii) *involvement of a technical panel to recommend as to possible candidates for a mutually acceptable expert(s) to assist in resolving difficult technical issues.—*
> Western Newfoundland model forest process — Ground Rules

### How does a voluntary process lead to more constructive negotiations?

Struggling with difficult issues where relationships have become strained is the "stuff of negotiation." Throughout the difficult moments of bargaining, the freedom to leave prompts parties to evaluate the benefits of staying. They will continually ask themselves whether their interests would be better served by being elsewhere and their best options if negotiations fail — what is sometimes called the BATNA or "best alternative to a negotiated agreement." Knowing this alternative gives each representative a baseline against which options under consideration can be measured. It is only meaningful if parties are free to pursue alternatives if negotiations fail.

This stage of negotiations also requires creativity and openness to new ideas, facts, and options. Again, parties are more likely to be so disposed when participation is voluntary rather than compulsory. No one is at his or her creative best when coerced.

Parties may find it useful at this stage to push the "voluntary" principle a bit further. Just as they first met on an understanding that no obligations were implied, they can set aside time for "invention without commitment." This allows them to brainstorm knowing that ideas, even the wild ones, will not lock anyone into a particular commitment. Similarly, it may be useful for parties to develop tentative agreements on particular issues, but leave these open to later reconsideration. For example, the following provision was made in the ground rules of the Saskatchewan Wildlife Diversification Task Force:

- *Members agree to operate by consensus which shall mean the agreement of all Consensus Members.*
- *In order to facilitate the broadest possible consideration of options and solutions, all suggestions and offers will be regarded as tentative until full agreement is reached. Understandings reached during discussions are interim pending agreement on a total package.*

This sort of arrangement allows each party to proceed in the confidence that they retain the freedom to reject a larger package at the end. By helping all representatives preserve their options as much as possible throughout the whole negotiating phase, it makes progress more likely.

### How does a voluntary process improve chances of successfully implementing the consensus?

The final stage of a consensus process is implementation. Agreements must now survive and operate in an outside world that is not necessarily sympathetic to or ready for the consensus the parties have endorsed. Chapter 10 explores in some detail the challenges of this ultimate and critical stage. Here, the question is how the voluntary nature of the process can help the agreement to be successfully carried out.

Free and informed participation provides two important benefits for implementation: commitment to the outcome and good working relationships. Both stem from basic human psychology. The decisions we are most committed to are those in which we participate most fully and freely. This is as true for groups as it is for individuals. If participation is coerced, the decision is not really ours and we remain ready to distance ourselves rapidly from any difficulties that arise in implementation. Conversely, if we enter an agreement freely, we bear responsibility for its fate and implications and so strive to make it work.

The relationships among parties can be critical to successful implementation. Reaching agreement is an overriding objective of the consensus process, but equally important is development of a positive, durable, and ongoing relationship between the parties. Again, voluntariness is a key to good relationships, while conscription is at best a shaky foundation. Understandings among parties who are forced to work together tend to be superficial compared to those that develop when parties want to cooperate.

## Conclusion

This chapter has traced the principle of voluntary participation throughout the four generalized stages of a consensus process. Getting to the table, talking about how to talk, dealing seriously with the issues through negotiations, and the crucial step of implementation depend on observing this principle. The second stage, in which parties talk about how to talk, provides a critical opportunity for them to capitalize on the advantages of a voluntary process and build in safeguards to uphold the principle. Ultimately it is the freedom to participate or not that gives a consensus process its integrity and its strength. The parties must work to preserve the voluntary nature of participation through the consensus process and beyond to implementation.

# Chapter 4
# Designing Consensus Processes

## PRINCIPLE 4: Self-Design

**The parties design the consensus process.**

"All parties must have an equal opportunity to participate in designing the process. There is no 'single' consensus process. Each process is designed to meet the circumstances and needs of the specific situation.

An impartial person, acceptable to all parties, can be an important catalyst to suggest options for designing the process, but ultimate control over the mandate, agenda, and issues should come from the participants themselves.

Designing a consensus process enables the participants to become better acquainted before they deal with difficult substantive issues.

It is important to take time at the beginning to

- define the issues clearly;
- assess the suitability of a consensus process for each issue — as opposed to other decision-making processes;
- clarify roles and responsibilities for everyone involved;
- establish the ground rules for operating.

Communications can be helped by establishing ground rules up front, and allocating time for the participants to appreciate each other's values and interests."

— *Building Consensus for a Sustainable Future: Guiding Principles*

Consensus processes offer parties many options for structuring their dialogue and problem solving. This flexibility is one of their advantages compared to more conventional, rule-driven approaches. However, negotiations are almost certain to fail if parties do not take care at the outset to define and agree upon a structure for the process. An initial set of shared expectations and understandings will provide the foundation on which to base all further discussions.

This chapter looks at issues parties must confront in designing a consensus process that meets their needs. After outlining why parties should design the process themselves, the chapter discusses the ground rules needed to shape the entire consensus process. It examines the issues involved in designing rules about who will participate, what the negotiations will focus on and seek to resolve, how the negotiations will actually be carried out, and the logistical issues of where and when things will be done.

## Why self-design?

The question "Why self-design?" really has two parts. First, why is a design needed at all? And, second, why should the parties do it themselves when there are well-known, off-the-shelf rules that they could quickly adopt?

The answer to the first question is that without some structure, misunderstandings abound and critically important steps and issues may get lost in the confusion. Indeed, many people dislike meetings, even when they take place within the bounds of a single organization where participants share a unifying purpose. The difficulties are that much greater when a problem-solving group consists of representatives from distinct and often adversarial organizations. Not only their meetings but also the larger context within which they meet are fraught with conflicting values, purposes, and understandings.

Negotiating groups made up of multiple and diverse stakeholders need a "constitution" that specifies

- how they will interact (rules of procedure),
- why (the objective),
- what (the issues that are and are not up for discussion),
- who (the parties who should be at the table), and
- when and where (the schedule and logistics).

Without agreement on such matters, there can be no process. Parties who assemble more than once without a framework that bounds the procedures and substance of their discussion are likely to become rapidly disenchanted and break off talks.

In light of the fact that there are existing formats for multiparty consensus processes, why not adopt an off-the-shelf model? There are several reasons for not doing so. First, this would sacrifice the important learning opportunity that self-design offers. Most groups and their representatives are unfamiliar with consensus processes. Working through questions of how, what, who, and so forth provides critical insights on how consensus differs from conventional processes. For example, in considering what they will talk about, parties may begin to see the difference between staunchly held positions ("under no conditions will we accept that facility here") and interests ("we are primarily concerned with the safety of our families and the effects on our property values").

A second reason why self-design is preferable arises from the special nature of every struggle over sustainability. These are extraordinarily complex and value-laden situations with unique personalities. They vary in such features as the number of significant players, the relative power of the key interests, the state and significance of scientific knowledge about the "facts," and the length of the dispute. Conventional ways of making environmental decisions allow comparatively little room to make the process fit unique aspects of the case. By contrast, consensus offers the opportunity to adapt the rules to the situation. This can prove especially valuable when parties come from vastly different social and cultural backgrounds, since it allows the invention of hybrid approaches that are as consistent as possible with all parties' needs and expectations.

Another somewhat more tactical reason exists for groups to work through the issues of process design. It provides a first opportunity for becoming acquainted and discovering that cooperation is actually possible — or that it is not possible. If the parties simply plunge immediately into negotiations, at best there will be a flurry of disjointed suggestions on what to do, stemming from the undisclosed self-interests of each speaker. Even worse, the discussions can degenerate into an exchange of accusations. Breakdown is predictable in an atmosphere that is just as hostile as the world outside the consensus forum.

Substantive issues may be too highly charged and divisive to start on, especially for people who are unfamiliar to and angry with one another. Talking about process may still bring up controversial issues, but the focus can be on matters that are generally less charged. On the safer ground of this agenda, an opportunity exists to get to know one another, make a few relatively harmless mistakes, and develop a better way of interacting. At this stage, it is often useful to get help from a neutral convenor experienced in establishing consensus processes. For example, in the Western Newfoundland model forest process and in the Saskatchewan Wildlife Diversification Task Force — both of which involved a broad range of stakeholders with

little experience working with one another — a professional mediator was brought in to conduct a workshop on ground rules. As a result, participants were able to cooperate successfully in designing their own process and gain more confidence in the subsequent negotiations.

A final reason for a self-designed process is that people tend to respect rules more when they have had a strong hand in establishing them. Later, if problems arise, the parties have an agreed-upon base for resolving differences.

### How can ground rules shape a consensus process?

This section focuses on what "design" issues can and should be addressed through agreement on ground rules. The issues are discussed in terms of the familiar questions: who, why, what, how, where, and when? Issues not dealt with here are covered in other chapters and cross-referenced as appropriate.

### Ground rules about "who?"

One of the basic difficulties in establishing a consensus process is determining who should be at the table (see Chapter 2 on the importance of inclusiveness). Further, as the parties who constitute an initial consensus group begin their work, they may wish to make some immediate additions. Certainly, they need to spend time assessing the completeness of their team and, through ground rules, establish a margin for error. (Chapter 3 outlines some options for dealing with "late entries" and provides examples of potentially useful ground rules.)

Ground rules usually specify exactly who is at the table and in what capacity. Sometimes distinctions may be made between those whose agreement is formally required for full consensus and parties who attend primarily to observe. Ground rules can also identify groups who have chosen not to participate but with whom regular communication is to be maintained. The means for doing this can also be specified.

Ground rules also need to address the important question of who else can attend. Options run from completely open meetings, through attendance by prior notice or invitation, to purely in camera sessions. In the Western Newfoundland model forest process, the meetings of the full committee are pre-announced and open to the general public. The Alberta-Pacific Forest Management Task Force also put a high value on openness, but felt that some prior indication of attendance was needed for logistical reasons. It also wanted to ensure that the presence of non-members would not discourage members from speaking freely. The Task Force's solution was to adopt a rule that non-members could attend only when invited by a representative. As the process evolved, enforcement of this rule was relaxed.

The choice of how open to be is difficult. An open-door policy may create problems of keeping order and discourage free speech. It may lead some representatives to grandstand for the sake of an audience rather than work seriously and consider compromises. Closing the doors, on the other hand, may undermine public confidence in the process and breed suspicion. Representatives and their constituents must carefully balance these considerations when designing their process.

Discussions of ground rules governing who should participate should also address the roles and responsibilities of the representatives. For example, representatives may differ significantly in how far they can commit to emerging agreements without checking back with constituents. Some representatives must go back for interim approvals throughout a process. Others have considerable leeway, and ground rules can make it their responsibility

to decide whether and at what points to consult with constituents. Ground rules should accommodate each representative's situation. In the Sandspit harbour process, the guidelines stated:

> *The Parties are proceeding on the basis that what is said or done by the Representative of the Principal Participants in the mediation process is reasonably believed by the Representative to reflect, or is likely to reflect, the concerns, wishes and interests of the party whose interests they represent, and where there is uncertainty as to whether that is the case, to make that known.* — Sandspit harbour process — Ground Rules

## Ground rules about "why?"

When parties design their process they will need to be clear on precisely what they seek to accomplish. The answer may seem obvious: total agreement on what to do about whatever is at issue. But it should be remembered that many participants may be unacquainted with the philosophy and definitions of consensus building. They may still expect some form of vote on the final resolution or, if there is a process manager, expect that he or she will make the final decision. A consensus group can best handle these sources of confusion by defining exactly what they understand by "consensus" and how, exactly, they will know when they have reached it. (Some sample definitions appear in Chapter 3, Box 3-1.)

Chapter 3 argued that it is unwise for groups to expand the meaning of "consensus" and accept less than unanimous agreement. They may wish, however, to frame ground rules enabling them to reach useful partial understandings on some issues while agreeing to disagree on others. Here is an excerpt from the applicable ground rule used in the Sandspit harbour process:

> *Should the Participants reach a consensus that resolves most, but not all, of the issues they may agree upon a Statement describing the areas of disagreement and any lack of information or data that prevents such agreement and where possible a process for achieving agreement on such issues. —* Sandspit harbour process — Ground Rules

Parties are, of course, free to include decision rules other than consensus if they make this explicit at the outset. Thus, for example, a group may decide to refer certain kinds of issues, especially complicated scientific questions, to outside experts and let them decide on the "facts."

Integral to thinking about *why* the process has been convened are questions about how committed parties will be to acting upon agreements. For example, it is sometimes the case that government regulatory agencies join consensus processes believing they can participate actively while reserving the right to revise the agreement later.

## Ground rules about "what?"

Ground rules about "what" concern the potentially conflicting views the parties often have on what issues to address in order to reach final agreement. People caught up in emotionally charged controversies frequently have significantly different versions of the issues. As they begin to negotiate, parties need to agree on and record a single, concise statement of exactly what issues they intend to resolve. They may also wish to specifically exclude some issues — ones outside their competence to resolve or irrelevant to the main issue. In the Alberta-Pacific forest

management negotiations, there was early agreement not to address outstanding concerns about the company's pulp mill in a forum dedicated to timber harvesting issues. The negotiating team also concluded that the unique jurisdictional concerns of Aboriginal participants would be better addressed in a parallel process, involving only relevant players.

There are no firm rules for deciding what is on, or off, the agenda. Sometimes it is useful to include as many issues as possible, even ones that seem remotely related to the key topics. This may provide "tradeable" issues that can be used to make a "package" settlement (one with something for every interest) easier to devise. At other times, it is wiser to restrict the agenda to the most pressing issues within the mandate and competence of the negotiators. This judgement call is often the most important one facing parties who are designing their consensus process.

## Ground rules about "how?"

Parties have many decisions to make regarding how the process is to be run. Among these are decisions about

- standards of conduct and behaviour during the negotiations,
- media relations,
- confidentiality,
- provision and sharing of expertise and information,
- records of discussion, and
- resourcing the process.

The following discussion outlines some options available for dealing with these issues.

*Rules of conduct:* There is a widespread belief that some of the most ordinary protocols and courtesies of human interaction can be suspended when people negotiate. Personal attacks, unreasonable demands, threats, and secrets are deemed normal negotiating behaviour. But there is a growing shift from this hard, positional bargaining philosophy to one based on candid, honest, and non-coercive communication. Some groups choose to incorporate the key concepts of this more "principled" approach to negotiations explicitly within their procedural rules. For example, the Western Newfoundland model forest process established the following norms as part of its ground rules:

> *The Members agree to act in "good faith" in all aspects of the process.... The Members accept the concerns and goals of others as legitimate.... It is important that a Member raises with the Management Group any matter which they perceive to be in violation of these ground rules or of "good faith" consensus building.... The focus will be on interests and concerns rather than on demands and positions.... The Members commit to fully explore issues, searching for solutions in a problem solving and consensus building atmosphere.... The Members will refrain from personal attacks and characterizations.* — Western Newfoundland model forest process — Ground Rules

Rules of conduct should also set out expectations regarding regular attendance. It is extremely disruptive and a waste of other members' time when key actors fail to attend. Frequently, consensus groups design quite stringent requirements to assure attendance and consistent representation. Ground rules may also provide for limited use of alternates. When such substitutes are allowed, means must be found to ensure they are well briefed and therefore do not hold the process back.

*Media relations:* The press can be invaluable in making sure that a consensus process gets information out to the public; but media coverage can also deepen misunderstandings if coverage is incomplete or inaccurate. During a consensus process, discussions frequently require both candour and delicacy. Achieving this in the full glare of the media may be extraordinarily difficult, especially when the press focuses on controversy and neglects the less newsworthy achievement of cooperation.

Several options exist for addressing the challenge and opportunity of media relations:

- Devise clear guidelines on communications with the press by individual representatives: often, groups agree they will not discuss other parties' views or "live" issues with the media.
- Designate one spokesperson whose communications will be guided and monitored by the rest of the consensus group; sometimes a mediator can be assigned this role.
- Prepare regular summary statements and press releases; time can be allotted at the end of each regular meeting to write a public announcement.
- Hold frequent public sessions and be honest in informing both the press and the public of discussions that are necessarily in camera; many people understand that negotiations require some confidentiality if they are otherwise well informed.
- Prepare and circulate information kits to the press at specified milestones within the process.

Groups can also write newspaper articles, which may best be submitted as paid advertising, to ensure accurate representation of complicated issues. In the Sandspit harbour process, working groups prepared a five-part sequence of full-page question-and-answer articles, which were reviewed by the full team, and then placed in the local newspaper. The Saskatchewan Wildlife Diversification Task Force adopted the following ground rule:

- *A summary statement suitable for discussion with the media and general public may be agreed upon and prepared at the conclusion of each Task Force meeting as a formal statement describing the progress of the Task Force. A subcommittee may be formed to assist in that activity. In discussions, the Task Force Members will respond within the spirit of this joint summary.*
- *Task Force Members will not characterize the positions or suggestions of other Members in their discussions with the public or the media.*
- *The meetings will be closed. —* Saskatchewan Wildlife Diversification Task Force — Operating Rules

*Confidentiality:* Closely related to the challenge of media relations is the confidentiality of consensus proceedings, internal memos, and so forth. Again, each consensus process will be subject to a different mix of forces pushing the group toward or away from full disclosure. Often, there are legitimate concerns that comments and tentative offers made as part of the negotiations not be taken out of context or in some way used against the parties later, for example, in future litigation. Such concerns can stifle the most imaginative concepts and innovative solutions.

Consensus teams may decide to include specific disclaimers in their ground rules to avoid this. The following is an example from the Saskatchewan process:

*Information provided, statements, positions and offers made during the process should be understood as being made only for the*

*purposes of the process and not as binding for any other purpose including litigation and administrative procedures and other activity or to attempt to bind any other participants or person in any such forum. —* Saskatchewan Wildlife Diversification Task Force — Operating Rules

A consensus group setting rules of confidentiality should ensure these do not conflict with applicable laws and regulations. If, for example, negotiations are taking place in the context of a provincial environmental assessment act, there may well be freedom of information requirements that render a confidentiality protocol invalid.

Even when it is not possible, legally or for fear of public reaction, for parties to maintain strict confidentiality around discussions, they may still be able to achieve the atmosphere needed for trying out new ideas and positions. Informal working groups can be established to come up with draft concepts. These groups are much less likely to attract wide public attention even when they meet openly. Indeed, because of the draft status of whatever they conclude, working groups can be excellent opportunities for involving people from outside the full consensus process.

*Information and expertise:* The complexity of many public disputes requires the development and use of much technical information. This poses a number of challenges that should be addressed in the ground rules. For example, ground rules should spell out the responsibility of parties to provide the information necessary for proper assessment of potential agreements. Proprietary information may be involved, particularly where private sector organizations participate in the process. It may be necessary to agree on procedures for "sanitizing" such information by aggregating data, deleting irrelevant data, or providing the information to a mutually acceptable third party for analysis. Chapter 6 discusses the importance of competent expertise on technical issues. Ground rules can help ensure efficient use of experts and prevent situations of "your Ph.D. against mine." Box 4-1 presents the relevant ground rules used in several consensus processes.

*Records of discussions:* All problem-solving groups need to keep track of what has been accomplished. However, taking and reviewing formal minutes can have a chilling effect. For one thing, negotiators may worry about having to defend something said in a purely speculative manner. Formal adoption of minutes also can reopen issues that had been settled. For these reasons, in designing their approach to record keeping, consensus groups mostly opt for informal and non-specific means. Negotiators can make notes for their own use, but these should be specified as having no official status and ground rules should preclude their use in any subsequent legal or administrative proceedings. Meeting notes can still be prepared, distributed, and double-checked by the group. These informal notes on the negotiating sessions can summarize the general topics discussed, agenda items for future meetings, tasks to be accomplished by individuals and subgroups, and important dates and deadlines.

*Resourcing the process:* Consensus processes have costs both for the group as a whole and for individuals. Some members have far fewer resources than others and may need assistance if they are to participate fully. Careful assessment of collective and individual needs at the outset is an important but often overlooked element in the self-design of the process. Misunderstandings over who pays for what and about the implications of one party "footing the bill" can create serious divisions

among members, as well as between them and the organizations they represent. Some citizen groups, for example, may be concerned if a developer whom they oppose covers their representatives' expenses. Yet, in more and more cases, the project proponent is paying for review processes — including the costs of involving critics. When designing their processes, consensus-building groups need to wrestle with the trade-offs around such issues and come to a written understanding on rules that apply.

## *Ground rules about "where?" and "when?"*

Finally, even in the most straightforward process, consensus teams will need to specify where they will meet, how often, and when. This apparently simple matter can become contentious. Less well-financed participants and those not being paid to attend may have more difficulty than others with the scheduling and location of meetings. It is much easier for representatives who are "on the job" and have an expense account to accept cancellations or the need to travel to remote locations for meetings. Problems can also arise if significant events for one party are unknown to others. For example, a negotiation session may be called during prime fishing season in a process involving a First Nation that relies on the fishery. This party's response may be: "Why are they trying to hold this meeting when all our leaders are likely to be away?" In cross-cultural settings in particular, resentment and suspicions about manipulation may be provoked quite inadvertently. Early discussion and agreement on the location and schedule of meetings can help prevent this.

Setting deadlines both for interim goals and for an overall consensus is an especially crucial step for parties in the design of their process. Time limits energize participation and provide

**Box 4-1**

# Sample Ground Rules on Information and Expertise

### Alberta-Pacific Forest Management Task Force

"It is established as a principle that all participating caucuses should have independent access to expertise necessary to review and evaluate data and proposals.

- technical support funds will be provided to enable the Task Force to mutually select those with the expertise necessary to develop data, interpret and verify information and generate alternatives at the request of the Task Force.

- funds to enable any caucus to verify information or data supplied by a consultant, expert or staff of the Company shall be made available to any caucus with the concurrence of the Task Force.

- in the interest of finding mutual agreements and solutions an individual caucus arranging the services of an expert under this provision will seek to identify experts with the broadest possible credibility with other Task Force members. It is established as a principle that all participating caucuses should have independent access to expertise necessary to review and evaluate data and proposals." — *Task Force Procedures*

### Sandspit Small Craft Harbour Mediation Process

"Any Party, at its expense, may use such expert assistance as it may consider appropriate and any direct involvement of such expertise in any mediation meeting shall be after prior notification of the other Principal Parties and the Mediator. If expert assistance in a particular field, or in respect to a particular subject matter, is seen as a matter of mutual interest to the Principal Participants, and potentially helpful to the mediation process, and consensus can be reached as to the expert whose advice is to be relied upon or with whom consultations would be helpful, then such expertise shall become a Cost of the Process. ...

All Parties agree that they will supply whatever information and data that it reasonably considers will be helpful in resolving the issues and to make it available on a timely basis, and, specifically to provide any information which is referred to or relied on in the mediation process." — *Ground Rules*

### Western Newfoundland Model Forest Process

"At an early stage in the consensus building process, the Management Group will develop a common information base, identifying areas where available information needs to be shared and/or verified, additional interpretation is required or additional information is required... Requests for information will be coordinated through the Management Group and/or the General Manager." — *Ground Rules*

an opportunity for self-assessment. But they also can become the source of frustration and controversy when missed. This subject is taken up at length in Chapter 9, which points out the need for agreement on firm initial targets and for flexibility in revising these as needed.

## *Ground rules about the mediator*

Finally, if a mediator is engaged in the process, the parties should confirm in ground rules their common understanding about this person's role and responsibilities. There are several key issues that should be discussed and agreed upon:

- Is the mediator to be present throughout the process or brought in only when impasses develop? Parties need to think about the management needs of the entire process.
- How does the mediator "take orders?" Care is needed to avoid situations in which one of the parties demands that the mediator do something without the agreement of all participants in the process.
- Who pays for the mediator's services? Parties need to talk about the appearance as well as the reality of the mediator's impartiality and the importance of disclosing how the mediator is to be paid (particularly if parties are not going to share the costs equally).
- What role might the mediator play as a spokesperson, for example, to the media, and what kind of "pre-clearance" might be needed from the negotiators? To avoid serious misunderstandings, the timing and authority must be clear regarding any information the mediator conveys on behalf of the group.
- Should there be restrictions on the mediator's ability to meet separately or jointly in caucuses with the parties? Are

there other acceptable ways of giving special assistance to individual parties (e.g., attending meetings of a party's constituency to help explain emerging aspects of an agreement)? As discussed in Chapter 6, equalizing the "resources" of different parties and making sure that each participates as best it can may require special attention from a skilled mediator; this role needs to be well understood by all parties to avoid any perception of special treatment.

- What, if any, responsibilities does the mediator have after final agreement and ratification occur? The parties may wish to specify a role for their mediator in dispute resolution during the implementation phase

See Appendix 2 for an overview of the tasks of the mediator in a complex public dispute.

## Conclusion

Each of the familiar planning questions — who, why, what, how, when, and where — leads to further issues that powerfully influence the course and success of a consensus process. In each case, groups face serious problems if they fail to talk about choices and reach agreement on what is appropriate to their situation. Such agreement is best accomplished at the outset. This is not to say that the parties should cast their rules and procedures in stone. Indeed, the next chapter is about the importance of maintaining flexibility throughout the process, and this applies equally well to process design. However, as explained above, solid and shared understandings are essential, particularly during the early, difficult stages of negotiation. Formulating ground rules gives parties control over the process and helps them understand the complexities they will face in building a consensus.

# Chapter 5
# Keeping Consensus Processes Flexible

## PRINCIPLE 5: Flexibility

### Flexibility should be designed into the process.

"It is impossible to anticipate everything in a consensus process. By designing flexibility into the process, participants can anticipate and better handle change when it faces them.

A consensus process involves learning from the perspectives of all participants. Feedback must, therefore, be continually incorporated into the process.

Flexibility is important. The initial design may evolve as the parties become more familiar with the issues, the process, and each other."

— *Building Consensus for a Sustainable Future: Guiding Principles*

In most forums for resolving sustainability issues, decisions unfold in a prescribed manner. Consensus building, in contrast, is not nearly so constrained. As emphasized in the previous chapter, stakeholders can tailor the process to their needs and circumstances. Furthermore, almost all the principal features of the process — parties, issues, facts, timing, and so forth — are subject to substantial change. The capacity to reconcile the process with new realities and significant surprises helps participants to maintain confidence and ownership in their process. This enables the process to focus constantly on the parties' primary interests.

This chapter explores how to build flexibility into a consensus process. It looks at how situations change during consensus building and why such changes need flexible responses. Next, it focuses on how participants can anticipate and make required changes without derailing the negotiations. Finally, it considers limits to flexibility.

The focus here is mainly on process flexibility. However, participants in the process also have to be personally flexible if they are to be comfortable with and competent in making adjustments to the process.

Probably the most important way in which parties need to be flexible is in their attitudes toward learning about and respecting the values and interests of other parties. (The importance of respect and understanding is considered in detail in Chapter 7.) They also need to be creative in reshaping images of the common problem and open to the views and suggestions of others. Negotiations are best understood as a continuous learning process in which parties come to know more about other parties and their interests, the "facts" of the situation, and even their own needs and values. Parties who are personally flexible in this sense are always more effective in contributing to a consensus settlement.

## What kinds of changes call for flexibility?

As negotiations begin, participants usually operate under the following assumptions:

- current representatives will continue to speak for their constituencies,
- all significant interests are represented,
- the issues have been well identified and defined,
- the parties have a good grasp of the facts of the situation,
- the outside world will stay much as it is for the duration of the process,
- the time needed to accomplish specific tasks and reach final agreement is known and sufficient,
- the parties will ultimately find grounds for a settlement acceptable to one another and their constituents; that is, a solution is within reach, and
- if an agreement is concluded, implementation can proceed as laid out in a final settlement plan.

These assumptions are not necessarily naive. To start and continue with difficult negotiations, parties need some confidence in all these matters. They develop these working assumptions by carefully assessing prospects for success before coming to the table and through self-design of the process. However, as the following discussion suggests, any of the above assumptions may unravel as the process unfolds.

### Representatives change

Consensus processes require representatives to participate in a variety of activities — discussion, analysis, fact finding, brainstorming, public briefings, and negotiations. Over time, the group acquires a certain persona as people find ways to work together. But while continuity of representation is desirable, it may not always be possible. For example, negotiators may cease to work for the agency they represent or a party may decide to change its negotiators.

The impact of changes in representation can be substantial. New faces at the table may disrupt the "style" of discussions or violate subtle and unspoken rules of discourse that have grown up among negotiators. Newcomers may also have difficulty grasping the details and nuances of all that has happened so far. They need the opportunity to assimilate all this information and, understandably, may challenge previous decisions. The original participants will be concerned about delays and possible demands from newcomers for reopening previously settled issues. Like other kinds of changes, changes in representation raise difficulties that, in the absence of a flexible response, can disrupt the entire consensus process. In developing initial guidelines for the process, the parties can develop measures to "break in" new representatives.

### New parties emerge

The evolving consensus process may also bring forth new parties. Sometimes a previously "outside" group is only identified or becomes aware of the process after it has begun. Or it may be that as the defined boundaries of the problem shift, new stakeholders emerge. When mediated negotiations began in the Sandspit harbour case, attention centred entirely on one particular site for the project. As discussions proceeded, the parties had to consider alternative locations. When several new sites became serious candidates, parties whose interests were now potentially affected came forward. These included occupants of neighbouring homes and a "stream enhancement" group concerned with the effects of one new location on a nearby stream.

For a consensus process to continue to be effective, there must be a flexible response to the emergence of new stakeholders along the way. Ignoring these groups is unwise since, although they may not have a right to participate in negotiations, they may have the power to block implementation.

### Issues broaden or change in priority

The learning that occurs within a consensus process often challenges initial definitions of key issues. As problems come into sharper focus and begin to evolve, the process may need to be adjusted to respond to new priorities. At the beginning of the Sandspit negotiations, for example, most participants believed their task centred on devising a way to avoid impacts on fish and waterfowl. When relocating the project became an option, the relative socio-economic benefits of different sites became a central question. The negotiators now had to talk about matters that had not previously been considered.

The boundaries of the issues may also enlarge: a group debating the expansion of an existing landfill site may see that some interests cannot be satisfied without a regional strategy for reducing waste that would allow the landfill to be phased out. Or an Aboriginal group may meet with fisheries agencies to talk about enforcement problems and end up discussing conservation issues. Consensus processes must offer the flexibility to reframe issues as they evolve.

One of the surest ways to prepare for changes that may come about in issues and priorities is for the negotiators to have an explicit understanding on what will not change through the process, such as broad goals and principles. These become a stable foundation that allows the participants to be flexible while still upholding the things that matter most to them, individually and collectively.

### Disputes arise over "facts"

Consensus building in the context of sustainability issues is characterized by great complexity and continuous inputs of scientific information. When parties begin to negotiate there is usually a fragmented information base and many versions of reality. During the process, new information comes to light. Old "facts" lose their certainty. A debate over the impact of development on a rare bird may be illuminated (or complicated) by new data on the species' geographic range. Controversies over health risks are continually transformed by rapidly evolving information on the effects of exposure to toxic substances. Thus, fundamental concepts and claims about the situation, how it came about, and how it may be affected by alternative actions are subject to radical change.

At the extreme, parties may be tempted to put off a consensus process on the grounds that a better, even conclusive, resolution of their differences awaits the completion of a study. But science is rarely able to provide such finality. Parties generally find they can proceed with worthwhile negotiations amid continuing scientific uncertainty, using the process to develop the best possible shared "theory" about relevant facts. At the same time, they must remain open to new information that is bound to keep changing as agreement is reached. The process, also, must be sufficiently flexible to accommodate this information.

### Developments outside the process

Consensus processes do not operate in a vacuum. Frequently, they occur in the shadow of a court or some other decision-making body. For example, in 1990 the Supreme Court of Canada issued the Sparrow decision concerning the scope of traditional Aboriginal rights versus federal authority over fisheries. This decision affected negotiations on co-management of the resource that had been under way for several years between various First Nations and fisheries agencies. The process had to adapt to the changed legal basis for negotiations, and each side had to reconsider how to advance its interests.

Changing political environments and public opinion likewise can strongly affect negotiations. A change in government or sudden heightening of public concern following dramatic events, such as a major oil spill or high profile protest, can influence the negotiating environment. For the most part, these broad kinds of changes cannot be anticipated with any confidence. Yet, groups must expect — and prepare for — unexpected external events when establishing a consensus process.

### More time needed to complete tasks/final agreement

Any of the above changes can affect the time required for a consensus process to run its course. Generally, unexpected and significant developments will prolong the process. This can be divisive and discouraging, especially for parties who entered negotiations anticipating a rapid settlement. Parties can reduce the possibility of such disappointments by being flexible on deadlines. Chapter 9 explores more fully the difficult trade-off between the need for flexibility and the benefits of staying within agreed time limits.

### Impasse and doubts over the feasibility of settlement

Despite sincere efforts, impasse does happen. The problem may stem from insufficient creativity or resources. Constituencies may refuse to give up long-held positions despite being presented with what negotiators believe is a reasonable proposal. Ultimately, there may be no choice but to end the process without agreement. Although this happens, a flexible response to imminent breakdown in negotiations can salvage the process itself or some substantial gains made during the process. It can also preserve the constructive relationships built up during the process that may help parties resolve their differences at a later time.

### Problems during implementation

Once constituencies have ratified a final consensus, parties too often believe implementation will unfold smoothly. But despite their best efforts at anticipating pitfalls, the implementation phase often encounters serious difficulties. Overcoming difficulties

that emerge during implementation often demands flexibility from all parties in applying their agreement.

## How can flexibility be achieved in a consensus process?

The following discussion explores ways of coping flexibly with the many kinds of change and uncertainty encountered in a consensus process.

### Representatives change

At the outset of a process, all representatives should commit to attending every meeting and to seeing the process through to conclusion. Representatives should inform the consensus group of any reasons why they may not be able to honour this commitment. A further precautionary measure is to appoint alternates — people who have the confidence of their constituents and who can substitute if the full member is absent or leaves the process. Ground rules can specify that full members keep alternates informed enough to be able to step in without interrupting progress. In some consensus processes, alternates attend all meetings even when the full member is present.

### New parties emerge

In complex negotiations, new and often only peripherally involved stakeholders may emerge to challenge the process. When potential participants ask for a seat at the table, it is often useful to explore whether a means other than direct representation could effectively meet their needs. Full membership is a big commitment, and potential participants may discover their concerns are already adequately addressed or even represented.

During the Sandspit harbour negotiations, for example, a community group in Sandspit became concerned that the project would be "voted down." Once this group discovered that decisions were based on consensus rather than voting, and because their community was already represented, they decided to remain outside the negotiations. Prospective parties may find that having an adequate opportunity to present their views makes full participation unnecessary. Consistent and clear media communications, special workshops and briefings, informal "town hall" meetings, and the inclusion of non-members as observers or members of working groups can provide sufficient involvement for many stakeholders.

In the Yukon land claims, a team of negotiators representing all negotiating parties regularly met with interest groups that were not at the table. These meetings opened up important two-way communications. Parties at the table were able to brief others about the evolution of agreements and to hear how other interests were affected by possible options for the agreement. These exchanges helped foster public support and build agreements that aimed to respond to a wide range of conflicting interests.

When these measures are not enough, new members must join negotiations. The addition of new members is easier if anticipated in the ground rules. In some cases, a consensus group may encourage the participation of new members. The Western Newfoundland model forest process, for example, established ground rules to permit easy access to the process for new members and also created an "open seat" for new stakeholders who might want to participate. When new members join a process, a mediator can play an important role by helping them become familiar with the guidelines and aware of the informal dynamics shaping the process.

### Issues broaden or change in priority

Issues may change in breadth or priority during negotiations, altering the original focus of discussions. When this happens, some parties whose primary interest lay within the initial focus may grow increasingly upset and even suspicious about the motives of other parties. Often nothing untoward is happening and anticipating this possibility should be considered when developing the ground rules. Periodic reviews of objectives and priorities, and of how time is being invested at the table, can remind negotiators of priorities and deadlines and enable them to make adjustments all can openly accept. Such reviews can preserve the necessary trust and good working relationships within the process.

### Disputes arise over "facts"

In complex environmental issues, disputes over facts are common. Often, a consensus process comes about for this very reason (see, for example, the proposed road extension at Lévis, Québec, described in Appendix 1). Parties should agree in advance on a procedure for resolving factual disputes. For example, parties may agree to bring in one or two experts to make presentations on the contested facts and answer questions from the parties. Alternatively, each side in a factual argument may select an expert, who then picks additional experts. The resulting panel studies and reports on the issue. The parties may agree in advance to be bound by the findings of an expert panel. Expert panels are frequently composed of outsiders, but they can also be made up of members within the process who have relevant technical knowledge.

### Developments outside the process

Two general strategies exist for dealing with external events that significantly affect the issues under negotiation. First, the consensus group can agree in advance to fully discuss any unexpected or upsetting development before any member acts in a way that could adversely affect the process. This reduces the risk of any member responding to an event with an ad hoc press release or taking a unilateral decision to withdraw from the process.

The second general strategy for coping with problematic external events is early detection. Flexibility is possible only when good information exists on what is happening "out there" that could affect the process. Such information can be gathered by setting aside regular times for discussing events outside the process. Often, the most potentially damaging changes occur in the constituencies of one or more of the parties. The better attuned each representative is to his or her constituency, the less chance any party will be caught off guard. Early in their work together, partners in the Western Newfoundland model forest process were able to respond effectively to a potentially divisive issue. When logging caused silting of a stream within the forest, the forest company representative alerted the other partners. The partners were able to work with the company in designing a special employee training program to prevent similar problems.

### More time needed to complete tasks/ final agreement

Often the time needed to resolve issues exceeds projections. This can be frustrating for negotiators whose constituents need an early decision, or who have been led by unrealistic deadlines to expect an early decision. Constant early reassessments of time limits help foster realistic expectations and enable deadlines to be adjusted in advance to minimize problems. Hard deadlines should be avoided early in the process, since this is the stage when a surprising amount of time is taken in building good relationships. Until the kinks have been worked out in a new process, time lines should be soft.

Later in the process, constituent demands for "real" results may be met by pre-implementing parts of the agreement. Any aspect of the agreement that all parties agree will go ahead regardless of agreement on other issues provides an excellent subject for pre-implementation. Such interim measures build confidence in the process and also help parties gain confidence in achieving a permanent settlement. Other options for managing time limits are discussed in Chapter 9.

### Impasse and doubts over the feasibility of settlement

Many mechanisms exist for breaking an impasse reached during negotiations. As discussed, working groups or outside experts can be brought in to resolve factual differences. The same approach can be used to find creative solutions to apparently intractable technical, social, or legal issues. Sometimes an outsider respected by all parties can provide a fresh perspective simply because he or she has some distance from the issues. A powerful new idea can often spark problem solving, as it did in one series of lengthy negotiations over mercury pollution of waters fished by local Indian bands. In this case, the parties were stalemated over how to compensate cases of mercury poisoning that might emerge well into the future. When someone proposed a permanent mercury disability fund, progress toward a settlement gained new momentum. The proposal enabled parties to break free from existing ways of looking at the issue and to focus on new ways to accommodate mutual concerns.

Parties may find it helpful to spell out a procedure for resolving potential impasses. This could involve mediation or referring the matter to a mutual third party for a non-binding opinion or to a meeting of the negotiators' principals. Having guidelines for referring disputes to the principals or an outside party provides a safety net around the process. Negotiators rarely want to admit outside help is necessary, and the existence of a last-resort process usually prompts the parties to work harder to solve differences.

Another approach to dealing with impasses involves anticipating in the ground rules the possibility that reaching a consensus may include agreeing to disagree on certain specific points. In the Saskatchewan Wildlife Diversification Task Force process, the ground rules provided for such a possibility:

- *Should Members reach a consensus that resolves most, but not all of the issues, they may agree upon a statement describing the areas of disagreement and any lack of information or data that prevents such agreement and where possible a process for achieving agreement on such issues.*
  — Saskatchewan Wildlife Diversification Task Force — "Operating Rules"

In the Saskatchewan example, the final recommendations acknowledged three issues on which no agreement was reached. However, the basis for the disagreement on those three items was clearly articulated. In relation to one potential pilot project in southern Saskatchewan involving non-resident big game hunting, a basis for assessing and considering it in the future was identified.

### Problems during implementation

The success of a consensus process is ultimately measured by results occurring well after a final settlement is ratified and signed. Chapter 10 details the ways negotiators can prepare to deal with the changes that take place after consensus is reached and which make implementation difficult.

## Are there limits to how flexible a process should be?

Flexibility should not be taken to mean that "anything goes." An infinitely flexible process would in the end not be a process at all, but merely a power struggle in which parties changed the rules to suit current objectives. An appropriate degree of flexibility entails careful consideration of reasons for changing the rules.

Some principles should be exempt from "flexibility." Being flexible on core principles is likely to create a far more difficult situation for the consensus process later on. Often great haste and missed deadlines cause parties to forgo what seem to be mere niceties of the process. When this happens, insufficient attention may be paid to achieving clarity and early agreement on ground rules (Principle 4); faulty assumptions about others' values and interests may be left to fester rather than revised in light of growing respect and understanding (Principle 7); representatives may neglect to consult frequently and in detail with their constituencies (Principle 8); or the special challenges of implementation may be inadequately discussed as a resolution is developed (Principle 10).

## Conclusion

Consensus processes are an attractive alternative to more rigid and rule-bound processes. Parties have the freedom to tailor a process to their situation and to reshape it when, predictably, the unpredictable happens. Moreover, the participants change as they learn more about the situation, about others, and about their fundamental self-interests. This learning precipitates constructive changes and builds better working relationships.

To respond positively to change, parties need to stay well informed about changing conditions throughout the process; they need to be creative in the range and kinds of adjustments they consider; they need to fashion ground rules in advance to guide them through the turmoil changes can impose; and they need, individually and collectively, to expect change and see it as a learning opportunity rather than a threat. In this way, an appropriate degree of flexibility can be attained.

# Chapter 6
# Providing Equal Opportunity for All Parties in Consensus Processes

## PRINCIPLE 6: Equal Opportunity

**All parties have equal access to relevant information and the opportunity to participate effectively throughout the process.**

"All parties must be able to participate effectively in the consensus process. Unless the process is open, fair, and equitable, agreement may not be reached and, if reached, may not last.

Not everyone starts from the same point — particularly in terms of experience, knowledge, and resources.

For example:

- the process involves time and expense — resources that not all participants can readily afford;
- the process revolves around the sharing of information on issues and impacts — something to which not all participants have ready access.

To promote equal opportunity consideration needs to be given to providing

- training on consensus processes and negotiating skills;
- adequate and fair access to all relevant information and expertise;
- resources for all participants to participate meaningfully."

*— Building Consensus for a Sustainable Future: Guiding Principles*

Compared with conventional adversarial approaches, consensus processes can ultimately be a faster and less expensive route to resolving disputes over sustainability issues. However, consensus processes are not without their own demands in terms of time, money, and other resources. The ability to meet these demands may vary substantially among parties. Groups who are short of funds, have limited access to information and expertise, or lack necessary bargaining skills, acumen, or power will have difficulty participating.

Unequal access to resources within a consensus-building group is a problem not just for under-resourced parties; it is a problem for everyone at the table. If any stakeholder's opportunity to participate is impeded, the benefits that fair and direct negotiations offer to all parties are lost. A superficial or false consensus may be arrived at and the parties will end up with the same inadequate outcomes that would have existed without negotiations. What is more, they will have wasted their time, lost credibility with their constituencies, and, in all likelihood, soured public opinion toward consensus building in general.

This chapter focuses on the need to ensure that parties in a consensus process have sufficient resources to enable them to participate effectively. It identifies the most important resources and describes ways of redressing unequal access to those resources.

## What resources do parties need to participate effectively in consensus building?

The demands placed upon parties in first getting to the bargaining table and then being effective there can be understood in terms of three basic resource requirements:

- financial resources,
- technical information and specialized expertise, and
- negotiating skills and acumen and other organizational resources.

### Financial resources

Involvement costs money. Consensus building over sustainability issues typically takes several months if not longer. During this time there are meetings to prepare for and attend. These entail travel costs, lost wages or business earnings, material costs of preparation, and costs of information or expert help.

While, overall, consensus processes may be less costly than other ways of settling disputes, they can place an unequal burden on individuals and groups with limited funds. Citizen action groups and First Nations often do not have resources budgeted for participating in such an activity. In contrast, proponents of proposed large-scale developments usually have the resources needed to mount and sustain lengthy review processes. Government agencies may face tight and seemingly rigid budgets but are generally in a far better position than most non-governmental organizations to meet the costs of protracted involvement in a consensus process.

As the parties in the Alberta-Pacific forest management case considered entering mediation, such inequalities were especially visible. On one side was Alberta-Pacific Forest Industries Inc., a consortium backed by Mitsubishi, one of the world's largest corporations; on the other side were local volunteer-based organizations such as the Friends of the Athabasca and Aboriginal groups.

In the Sandspit harbour dispute, the project proponent was the Government of Canada, which had allocated millions of dollars to planning and implementing the marina. Local residents who opposed the project lacked a unified organization as well as the funds needed to sustain their participation through lengthy environmental reviews.

In these and many other cases of consensus building, lack of money was a major obstacle from the beginning for some of the participants. Ways to overcome this hurdle are outlined later in this chapter.

### Technical information and specialized expertise

Consensus processes can make more than financial demands on participants. Environmental controversies tend to turn on issues that require substantial inputs of specialized scientific knowledge. The Alberta-Pacific project area encompassed thousands of hectares of diverse habitat — coniferous and hardwood forests, river valleys, lakes, and bogs. This meant that the sheer quantity of disputable facts and theories was potentially enormous. In the course of negotiations, parties had to reflect on highly complex matters — dynamic interactions between moose, caribou, and wolves; theories of "island biogeography" (related to the controversial issue of how clear cutting differently sized blocks of forest affects species diversity), and the ecology of streams, lakes, and gravel pits. Some parties at the table were backed by many experts in ecology and resource management; others had limited information and no specialized training relevant to the disputed issues.

With all this diverse technical information surrounding the negotiations, non-experts and parties with little or no access to specialized knowledge can easily feel overwhelmed as they try to hold their own with stakeholders who do have expertise. Lack of specialized knowledge may effectively exclude some parties, or — and sometimes this is worse — non-experts may get trapped into debates that leave them looking foolish in the eyes of other parties or their own constituencies.

### Negotiating skills, acumen, and other organizational resources

Parties may also be mismatched in bargaining skills and experience and, more broadly, in their overall strategic abilities as organizational actors. Some may have had years of experience in public policy controversies. They know how to pull their case together and how to manage the myriad details of the process — public relations, personnel management, checking with their constituencies. Moreover, they are confident negotiators. Other parties through inexperience lack that savvy and confidence.

Parties also differ in how prepared they are as organizations. Some, whether from business, government, or the non-governmental sector, have their organizational "act" together. They have time-tested means of internal communication and well-established decision procedures. Other groups may be less adept in handling the challenges of urgent collective action to deal with the uncertainties, contingencies, and frustrations of a protracted conflict.

### Toward "equal opportunity" among parties in consensus processes

What can be done to redress imbalances in the resources needed to participate in consensus processes? Several effective techniques are discussed below and summarized in Box 6-1.

#### Dealing with significantly unequal financial resources

The techniques for redressing imbalances in financial resources are for the most part straightforward — at least in principle. Over the past 20 years in Canada, environmental groups have successfully argued that direct financial assistance is essential to effective participation in decision making. In some of the early forums reviewing the environmental aspects of major projects, these groups focused on "intervenor" funding. The main goal of such funding was to enable the groups to conduct research and retain expertise comparable to that of the proponent. The argument was well stated in a position paper

---

**Box 6-1**

## Some Techniques for Equalizing Resources within Consensus Groups

### Financial Resources

- Provide "block" intervenor funding
- Have project proponent reimburse direct meeting costs
- Provide honoraria to compensate for lost work/business time

### Technical Information and Specialized Expertise

- Provide intervenor funding for hiring expertise
- Develop protocols for full information sharing
- Create technical working groups
- Hire experts in service of full consensus team
- Provide a common information base

### Negotiating Skills

- Provide "how to" books for home study
- Offer special training workshops

### Organizational Preparedness

- Provide mediator assistance in establishing new groups for previously unorganized interests
- Provide financial and other assistance to less well-organized groups
- Use coalitions to pool resources and share tasks

of the Canadian Environmental Law Association:

> *This [intervenor funding] would enable citizens appearing at environmental assessment hearings to place themselves on a footing more equal to project proponents who, in the case of major projects, may have expended hundreds of thousands, if not millions, of dollars in preparation....[8]*

Reimbursement for the significant costs of direct participation has also been an important objective in discussions of intervenor funding. Some of the more important questions quickly become "who is to pay for these expenses?" and "what costs will be covered?"

In the Alberta-Pacific negotiations, the company was willing to pay the travel expenses of consensus group members whose participation was not part of their actual jobs. More difficulty arose with the use of honoraria, financial compensation for the time lost from employment or business. Both the company and the government had concerns that honoraria with a policy of maximum inclusiveness (see Chapter 2) could lead to uncontrolled cost escalation. Honoraria can also present difficulties for other participants. Some non-governmental organizations (NGOs) are sensitive to potential problems from their own constituencies if any money is accepted from the project proponent. The concern is that the taking of such money could be seen as co-option by the opposition. This illustrates the importance of having funding available; but it also underlines the care all parties must exercise when accepting financial support from the "other side."

### Dealing with unequal access to technical information and specialized expertise

As noted, one of the main reasons financially strapped groups look for intervenor funding is to bridge the expertise gap between them and better-funded players. The struggle for equal access to knowledge and expert advice has been a difficult one throughout much of the recent history of public involvement in Canadian environmental decision making. Although the advantages of broader participation in decision making were rarely contested, it took many years for the information needs of public interest groups to be addressed. Through the courts and administrative forums, some innovative ways have been found to fund information gathering and expert advice. As well, many environmental and First Nation organizations have gradually developed their own expertise and have created a network of scientific advisers willing to work inexpensively or adjust their fees to a client's ability to pay.

While these strategies for levelling the playing field are important, consensus processes themselves offer unique opportunities to deal with unequal information and expertise. For example, cooperative approaches to handling information needs can eliminate the expensive process of pitting experts against each other. Abandoning "adversarial science" allows all parties to develop a more sophisticated and shared appreciation of technical issues.

A range of options exists for collaborative handling of information needs. Perhaps the most straightforward is to make an explicit agreement on access to information. Parties used to the strategic use of information in negotiations may have difficulty accepting full disclosure, believing that concealment and deception are integral to negotiation. But experience suggests these tactics are unhelpful and unnecessary in building consensus on sustainability issues. Full disclosure and openness should be the basic operating principle in attempting to build a consensus. It goes beyond simply surrendering documents that opponents know about and demand: parties should try to identify all relevant information and then provide any material whose importance becomes apparent during discussions. As needed, rules can be devised to handle the small fraction of materials containing legitimately private and proprietary information.

Early in the Sandspit negotiations, the two lead federal agencies furnished the team with a complete bibliography of harbour planning studies. The mediation team then reviewed these documents, requesting those that at least one party felt were needed.

One of the procedures agreed to by the Alberta-Pacific Forest Management Task Force was the development of a common information base, which identified areas where available information needed to be shared and/or verified. As a result, when disagreements arose over issues that ranged from the ecological significance of the forest understorey to the effectiveness of forest harvest monitoring, parties could argue on an equal footing.

While access to information is vital, there are several other principles and methods that can help to assure "knowledge equality." The Sandspit harbour negotiations relied extensively on consultations with leading experts in areas affecting the settlement. These experts were retained on behalf of the entire group rather than as partisan "witnesses." In one instance, an expert was hired when important questions arose over the feeding habits of Brant geese, which were often seen near the proposed harbour site. Harbour proponents did not want to rely solely on the expertise of the well-qualified waterfowl biologist on the mediation team, since that person represented an agency seen as a leading opponent of the development. Thus the mediation team agreed to locate a "Brant expert" who had no previous contact with the issue. They were able to find an Alaskan biologist and to engage this person for a lengthy conference call during which all parties could ask for clarifications of the facts.

The Alberta-Pacific negotiation also used expert briefings to the entire team. For example, Alberta-Pacific's wildlife biologist made a detailed presentation on the company's ongoing ecological research. Another time, one of the environmental group representatives led a discussion on innovative concepts of "holistic forestry." Sessions such as this that mix experts with non-expert representatives can be enormously beneficial in several ways. First, they help people with no scientific training to become familiar with the language and concepts of specialized fields, using sources that are neither partisan nor suspect. Second, they help technical experts extend their own insights into the workings of complex natural systems as they listen to long-time residents of an environment. Once the proper spirit is achieved in pooling expert and "experiential" knowledge, remarkably rich versions of environmental processes become possible.

*Dealing with differences in negotiating skills, acumen, and other "organizational resources"*

Parties can vary widely in their negotiating skills, acumen, and degree of organizational preparedness for consensus processes. These imbalances must be addressed if negotiations are to lead to fair and durable settlements. The following discussion deals with effective ways to restore some balance among the parties in these areas.

*Negotiating skills:* The past 10 years have seen tremendous advances in practical understanding of skills and skill building for consensus. Excellent "how to" books have been published,[9] which can be made available as parties prepare for consensus processes. Home study of these can complement training workshops run specifically for groups that have limited experience in negotiation. In the Alberta-Pacific case, environmental and Aboriginal groups requested mediation workshops primarily because they knew that company staff had already had this kind of learning experience. Across Canada a growing number of for-profit and non-profit centres are delivering training in negotiation.

*Acumen:* Workshops can help parties to build specific skills, but a sense of strategy in the overall course of negotiations comes more slowly. It may take repeated experience in consensus processes to develop a strong understanding of the best ways to advance one's own interests while meeting essential needs of other parties. One way to expedite this learning is to have a mediator work with each party, as needed, on how to participate most effectively in the process. Doing so can mean assisting them on a range of matters: distinguishing between short-term and long-term interests and ensuring that both are adequately addressed; screening out unnegotiable stances and issues; coordinating internal matters on teams of negotiators; and assessing the consequences for each party's interests of not getting an agreement — the array of challenges is vast and is one reason why skilled mediators who have "been this way before" can be so important in improving every party's effectiveness.

Sometimes the mediator will find it necessary to work most closely for a while with groups that are having particular trouble in coming to grips with the demands of complex multiparty negotiations. This is not a matter of playing favourites with one side or another; it is part and parcel of the mediator's responsibility in assisting the parties to create an effective process. The key is that everyone fully understands how it is in their interests for each negotiator to have the ability to effectively represent his or her constituents.

*Organizational resources:* Consensus groups can differ widely in the extent to which they coalesce as working and coordinating organizations. Government agencies and corporate proponents tend, predictably, to be better organized than ad hoc groups formed primarily to challenge a specific development. Aboriginal groups differ greatly from one to another in this regard. Some environmental and conservation groups have many years of successful organization and collective action, while others have only recently begun to take on complex policy issues. As discussed earlier in this chapter, groups that are not well organized can be at a significant disadvantage in the demanding environment of multiparty consensus processes.

What can be done to help less well-coordinated groups begin to organize effectively? First, there may be a need to organize individuals with similar interests and concerns into a new umbrella group. At the beginning of the Sandspit mediation, many residents of the Queen Charlotte Islands worried about the potential environmental effects of a harbour. But no single NGO existed to represent this perspective. Once the initial consensus group became aware of this, it helped a prominent local bird-watcher establish the Sandspit Mediation Environmental Group. Subsequently, the mediator and representatives from another Islands-based organization (which included pro-harbour interests) worked closely with this group to ensure its basic organizational needs were met.

Another approach to ensuring basic organizational competence is coalitions. The maxim "united we stand, divided we fall" is particularly true for clusters of small, resource-poor groups who bring similar concerns and interests to consensus processes. In essence, representation on the Alberta-Pacific Forest Management Task Force was organized through a coalition of five caucuses representing many independent interests. This approach created an opportunity for small organizations to work together strategically and to share information and other tasks. A related method of dealing with less well-organized interests is to identify an existing umbrella organization. The Athabasca Native Development Corporation was identified by its member bands as a good avenue through which they could pool efforts in the Alberta-Pacific negotiations.

## What if the parties have unequal power?

It is often said that negotiations cannot or should not be pursued when a major imbalance exists in the power of the parties. Yet this "resource," if it can be called that, is much harder to come to grips with than the others discussed here. Power is a complex attribute made up of many factors — the resources already spoken of, the broad economic influence of some parties, differing access to politicians and the press, even the special power that comes from being a much weaker party whom stronger groups are reluctant to attack.

Power is more than the sum of tangible and obvious resources. Much depends on timing and on unpredictable changes in the public's attitudes. Parties who have few of the concrete resources needed to represent their interests effectively may through hard work or good luck garner public sympathy, which can be a significant "equalizer."

A stronger group may then recognize the wisdom of treating a weaker adversary in a fair and principled manner. When this happens, the empowerment of the disadvantaged group can sometimes become self-sustaining. Indeed, for an unacknowledged small organization, one of the most attractive features of participating in a consensus process lies in its recognition by more powerful parties; this gives the weaker party legitimacy — a key component of power. Suddenly, other parties and government agencies have to take this party seriously if its agreement and overall consensus are to be secured.

Once parties are at the table, another important factor comes into play that also tends to level the playing field. This is each participant's right to say no and, if necessary, threaten to withdraw from further discussions. This is not a threat to be made lightly or repeatedly; however, provided valuable work has been done and an agreement has become a shared goal, each party's "veto" helps to balance power within the consensus process. On the other hand, it is also worth reiterating a point made in Chapter 3: the power parties would have without the consensus process is not sacrificed by participation; it is "parked" outside only so long as the process endures.

With all these contingencies and nuances, it may be difficult for any group to assess in advance of negotiations whether there is enough equality among would-be participants in terms of overall power. Each group needs to develop awareness about the factors that make it and its adversaries more or less powerful. But sometimes the only way a group can determine whether its power is sufficient is to exercise it during consensus building.

## Conclusion

Inequality among parties within a consensus process is everyone's problem. This applies whether the imbalance is financial, in the relative information and knowledge of the parties, or in their skills, acumen, and organizational preparedness for the process. For various reasons, it may be difficult for adversaries to take responsibility for doing something about this inequality. A mediator may have an important role to play in assisting specific parties to be effective participants, and by so doing enhance the likelihood of the process being effective, which is in the interests of all parties.

# Chapter 7
# Respecting and Understanding Diverse Interests

## PRINCIPLE 7: Respect for Diverse Interests

**Acceptance of the diverse values, interests, and knowledge of the parties involved in the consensus process is essential.**

"A consensus process affords an opportunity for all participants to better understand one another's diverse values, interests, and knowledge. This increased understanding fosters trust and openness, which invaluably assist the participants to move beyond bargaining over positions to explore their underlying interests and needs.

Recognizing and addressing all relevant stakeholders' values and interests provides a basis for crafting creative solutions that are more likely to last.

Sometimes parties may be deeply entrenched in an intense conflict prior to a consensus process. Reaching a consensus agreement involves exploring and developing common interests despite differences in values."

— *Building Consensus for a Sustainable Future: Guiding Principles*

First Nation Representative: *We will own and control all traplines within our traditional lands. This is non-negotiable for us.*

Government Wildlife Manager: *No! Traplines are a public resource that must operate for the good of all. Traplines must be used to develop their economic potential, and you do not run them that way now.*

Representative of Non-Aboriginal Trappers: *Why should anyone get special treatment? Without the same rules for everyone, these guys are going to trap out all the wildlife of this region.*

First Nation Negotiator: *We have our own way of coexisting with the animals. Traplines are an important part of our culture. Even for those who work at a regular job, trapping with their family is their culture, their way of keeping connected to the land.*

and so on....

These are the sounds of different values, interests, and cultures clashing. In the absence of respect and appreciation for different perspectives, conflicts can escalate into entrenched positions, deepened by mistrust and misunderstanding. Shaped by adversarial processes, agreements if reached at all are often non-viable compromises, grudgingly supported by the parties. However, if disputing parties step back from the dispute to explore and appreciate their differing points of view, unexpected opportunities can emerge for fair and broadly supported resolution.

This chapter urges parties to take that step back. It begins by discussing the essential distinction between respecting values and interests and approving of them. The chapter, in emphasizing the importance of respect in consensus building, considers why it is generally so difficult in the midst of conflict to empathize with other interests. Finally, it reviews helpful strategies and techniques for developing respect and understanding within a consensus process.

## Does developing respect and understanding mean accepting and embracing others' values and interests?

Parties may be understandably concerned that developing respect and understanding requires endorsing an opponent's values. Must an environmentalist who has worked tirelessly for the protection of endangered species embrace industrial development as a worthy value? Must a non-native fisher join First Nations in their struggle for self-governance? Must forestry companies agree that a rare liverwort is as important as a stand of timber?

At the end of a successful consensus process, each party can sustain their values and the belief that opponents' values have less merit. What is required is not a conversion of values but a tolerance for other values and respect for the people who hold them. The goal is to try to develop outcomes that enable the parties to live together in spite of their differences, not to eliminate these differences.

## Why respect and understanding are vital to consensus building?

The importance of mutual respect and understanding is evident in the context of the following challenges in building an agreement:

- The negotiators must find a way to meet the needs of all parties despite what may seem a zero-sum situation (someone must lose in order for someone else to gain).

- In many environmental controversies, long and bitter struggles create an extremely tense atmosphere in which misunderstanding thrives — the parties have to "de-escalate" interpersonal and group tensions.
- To bargain effectively, the parties must establish cordial interpersonal relations and mutual trust.
- The parties need new and creative ways of thinking to resolve impasses.
- The negotiators must arrive at a settlement that all constituencies can accept, ratify, and support.
- A durable settlement requires developing and sustaining positive relations among the parties.

### Finding "non zero-sum" solutions

The search for ways to overcome opposing positions begins with the recognition that one party's gain is not necessarily another party's loss. In the trapline dispute that introduced this chapter, Aboriginal people were less interested in the economic returns from traplines than their importance in preserving a lifestyle. For them, traplines brought families together and reinforced cultural values and customs. For government, anxious to develop economic activities in small communities, the Aboriginal cultural use of traplines was seen as a principal source of revenue and employment. In a broader context, however, the Aboriginal cultural use of traplines offers benefits that both parties seek: helping to reduce the economic and social costs of crime, family breakdown, and substance abuse. These benefits indirectly address government interests, since providing rural employment also serves to reduce these economic and social costs. Taking the time to explore each side's underlying interests and gaining an appreciation of the larger picture can make many negotiations less of a zero-sum struggle.

### Turning down the heat

Unless tension and hostility can be reduced, little hope exists for eventually reaching consensus. Reciprocal recognition and respect for the values of other parties can reduce the intensity of conflict. Misconceptions of other parties' values or circumstances lead to faulty assumptions that distort the understanding of demands and expectations. Understanding differences can improve communication in a way that reveals common ground. The experience of carefully listening and being listened to, of having a long-time adversary acknowledge differences and similarities and of doing the same in return, introduces a better understanding of other participants as people, not simply as opponents or negotiators. This understanding enhances the capacity to search for and find common ground.

### Building interpersonal relations and trust in "bargaining"

Parties eventually reach a stage in a consensus process when they exchange offers and candidly explore difficult choices and trade-offs. Success at this stage depends on constructive interpersonal relations. Understanding and respecting differences may lead to friendship. More importantly, it can reduce the basis for enmity, which can block open and trusting assessments of new proposals.

Trust can be a powerful unifying force, merging parties with diverse interests in a cooperative search for solutions. Conversely, distrust can drive parties to intractable positions, severely hindering the search for mutually beneficial solutions. Mutual respect for different values and circumstances fosters trust, particularly if the legitimacy of these differences is openly acknowledged.

*Setting the stage for creative problem solving*

Mutual respect for differences removes significant barriers to cooperative problem solving. It reduces the chances that a dispute will become a destructive struggle over the legitimacy or priority of competing values. Resources are less likely to be directed to un-productive attacks on an opponent's credibility or to promoting initial and uncompromising positions.

Creative solutions emerge in environments where respect, trust, and a desire to find mutual benefits predominate. Respect for diverse interests and values helps make it possible for parties to pool their resources in search of cooperative and creative ways to resolve difficult problems.

As the Sandspit harbour consensus process began, there was much disagreement about the ecology of Brant geese. Environmental scientists and managers, although expert in the general biology of waterfowl populations, had scant data on how these geese lived in the area surrounding Sandspit. Local proponents of the harbour had observed the birds for years but had no systematic way of turning their observations into explanations and predictions useful in an impact assessment. As mutual respect evolved, the parties were able to pool what they knew and develop a much better common understanding of the "Sandspit ecology" of Brant geese.

*Understanding other parties' difficulties in getting approval from constituents*

In a consensus process, one or more parties may have difficulty in getting constituency approval for proposed solutions. These problems may stem from the unique values and conventions of a party's organization or culture. Respect for differing values and organizational structures can help fellow negotiators develop a realistic understanding of the difficulties other parties face in maintaining the trust of their constituencies.

*Enhancing the durability of agreement*

Respect and understanding can become even more important after an agreement has been reached. Implementing a negotiated settle-ment may reveal problems the negotiating parties did not anticipate. Necessary funding approval could be held up unexpectedly. Or technical difficulties, political changes, and any number of unforeseen events may threaten the life of an agreement. Will these "surprises" reopen previous hostilities or will the parties regroup and work constructively to resolve new problems? The capacity to cope with unforeseen difficulties depends largely on establishing mutual respect and trust during the consensus process.

## How do parties differ? What sorts of differences need to be understood and respected?

Respect and understanding begin by accepting that differences are real. A common and beguiling notion is that differences are illusory, that basically everyone really wants, needs, and values the same thing — and often that thing is money. Successful salespeople, no less than managers operating in world markets, know that appreciating and respecting personal and cultural differences can make or break a deal. In situations such as the trapline dispute, simplifying differences into money versus culture would quickly destroy any chance of finding common ground.

Parties can differ in several important ways. First and most fundamentally, they differ in their values and interests. In sustainability disputes, developers may place high value on what they define as "progress," a measurable economic improvement. An environmental group may see the integrity of natural ecosystems as the most fundamental value. During the Sandspit mediation, environmentalists learned that the value local proponents placed on a harbour stemmed from its potential to stimulate the depressed local economy. At the same time, Sandspit representatives came to appreciate why several wild species mattered so much to environmental groups and agencies. Clarifying these differing values and interests made all parties more tolerant of their differences.

Parties may also hold differing beliefs — their own set of explanations and predictions — about the facts and issues. Indeed, parties frequently disagree on what the main facts and issues are. In complex situations, these differences may not be obvious. Again in the Sandspit case, environmentalists believed the proposed harbour site was a unique habitat for one waterfowl species, while others at the table believed this species could and would use a much wider range of environments. In time, the parties were able to look at the facts together and agree the truth probably lay somewhere between these views. But this cooperation was only possible when each party understood the other's perspective and the basis for it.

Parties can differ in the circumstances shaping their perspectives and abilities. They have different constituents to represent, different reporting requirements, different resources to call upon, and different skills to employ. All differences must be appreciated, respected, and accommodated to ensure consensus agreements encompass all interests fairly.

In many environmental disputes in Canada, the parties also differ culturally. Parties from differing cultural backgrounds introduce more than the usual differences in values, interests, beliefs, and circumstances. Even the most ordinary issue can ignite cultural conflict based on painful historical events. A gesture of friendship in one cultural context may be seen as an insult in another. What is important for one party may be trivial to someone else. Cross-cultural misunderstandings heighten tensions and reduce the possibility of agreement.

An awareness of how significantly parties can differ in values, interests, beliefs, circumstances, and culture contributes enormously to creating good working relationships. Such awareness, combined with tolerance of and respect for differences, makes building consensus possible.

### What makes respect for and understanding of differences hard to achieve?

Why are respect and understanding often so hard to develop? What are the obstacles to establishing respect and understanding?

The assumption that everyone is the same often hinders the evolution of respect. Not seeing or acknowledging differences can be interpreted as disrespectful. Another obstacle stems from exaggerated views of how different parties are. In consensus processes set up during long and bitter disputes, environ-mentalists are often labelled as tree huggers, loggers are called rednecks, while regulators are variously seen as bean counters blocking needed development or as surreptitious bed-fellows of industry. Extreme characterizations of other parties flourish in the absence of opportunities for constructive personal contact. They prevent parties from seeing beyond stereotypes to find people with common interests and values.

Lack of understanding can be provoked prior to negotiations by parties voicing extreme positions or ultimatums: "Under no conditions will we alter our plan for this project" or "The proposed development is an environmental disaster in the making and completely unacceptable in any form." When parties present their values and interests as immovable positions, other parties dig in their own positions and abandon efforts to develop understanding and respect.

Developing respect and understanding for differences can be hindered when parties face severe external pressures to settle quickly. The work — which can be time consuming — of building respect and finding out what really matters to adversaries can seem an unaffordable luxury when a resolution is urgent. However, hastily concluded agreements can easily unravel in the pressure of the real world. Such agreements may settle but rarely resolve differences.

## What is required to generate respect for and understanding of differences?

Respect does not require adopting another party's values, nor does it require religious or cultural conversion. At the most general level it is sufficient to acknowledge differences and

accept other parties' right to be different. Three kinds of commitment made at the outset of consensus processes can substantially advance mutual respect:

*A commitment to show consistent respect:* Respect and understanding depend on consis-tently civil behaviour. Demonstrating genuine respect in all dealings shows a willingness to understand and accept differences. Mistakes and misunderstandings will happen, but can be turned into learning opportunities with prompt apologies and joint reflection on how to do better.

*A commitment to share knowledge and information:* Mutual sharing of information and insights about unique values and circum-stances invites parties to be open to each other. This is especially important in cross-cultural settings, where there is so much to learn about styles of communication, customs, and distinctive world views.

*A commitment to invest time:* It is essential to take the time to understand differences throughout a consensus process. Today's obsession for quick fixes and tight schedules makes it difficult to develop the needed level of respect and understanding. Genuine respect cannot be built mechanically or quickly. It grows among parties through time and effort. Furthermore, understanding and respect for differences are ever-moving targets: they require ongoing upkeep and continuous relearning.

Bearing in mind these broad needs for civil conduct, information sharing, and patience, what specific strategies exist for fostering respect and understanding among parties in a consensus process?

### Workshops to break down barriers between groups

Cross-cultural workshops are widely used in Canada to introduce non-Aboriginal people to the cultural values and circumstances of Aboriginal people. Often facilitated by an Aboriginal person, these workshops yield important information and insights. Such workshops need not be restricted to cross-cultural contexts. Similar approaches can be used to build understanding between disputing groups from the same culture. Parties from similar cultural backgrounds may differ immensely in basic outlook. For instance, business and environmental group leaders may share a common language and culture, yet their social, political, and economic circumstances can lead to profoundly different values. Joint information workshops to reduce the misunderstandings that hinder consensus building are best held, with all parties attending, before starting negotiations.

Skill-building workshops can help dissolve cultural and other intergroup barriers. Improving the active listening[10] skills of participants can be especially important in breaking down negative stereotypes. Especially in Western society, people spend a lot of time speaking and little time listening. This limits the ability to hear what other parties say and to appreciate what they face within their constituencies.

Bringing all the parties together before negotiations begin for an intensive training workshop on interest-based negotiations offers several advantages. The workshop gives all parties an opportunity to share a common learning experience. Negotiating parties come to know each other as fellow students, and personal interactions are not burdened by substantive differences. During the workshop, "people" relationships replace negotiating relationships, nurturing the initial growth of understanding, respect, and even friendship. Such a workshop also helps all parties discover the potential of the consensus-building option to adversarial negotiations. Equally important, the workshop stimulates the parties to consider how to design their own process for negotiations — a process that respects all their differing needs and values.

### Looking at issues from the other party's side

The greater the tension surrounding a dispute, the greater the tendency for parties to think their point of view is the only correct one. In such disputes, the need for parties to understand other parties' circumstances is particularly acute. Seeing a conflict from the other parties' perspectives — learning about their pressures, concerns, and difficulties — helps open minds to creative problem solving. Equally important, the effort may encourage a reciprocal effort from the other parties.

A number of techniques can be used to help each party see the world, at least temporarily, as others do. Among these are formal exercises of role playing, role reversal, and active listening. It can also be useful to have parties participate in a simulation designed specifically to mimic the principal features of the real conflict; this exercise heightens appreciation for the difficulties faced by opponents.

Another technique is to have parties prepare and discuss worksheets that outline their views of opponents' issues, values, and beliefs.[11] This potentially sensitive exercise can profit from the help of a neutral party (see the section on skilled mediators).

## Creating a written statement recognizing differences and respect for them

In some processes it can be useful to agree to and write down principles about respect for diverse interests and views. A set of common understandings on this and related matters was developed during the course of the work of the Saskatchewan Wildlife Diversification Task Force (described in Appendix 1). These principles illustrate the "common platform" this committee created and the principles reflecting awareness and respect for diversity.

## Working groups to provide opportunities for greater openness

Complex consensus processes often form subcommittees or working groups to carry out tasks such as sifting through technical information, developing a media strategy, or developing options for specific parts of an agreement. In the Yukon land claims negotiations, a wildlife working group was able to break through many differences in developing proposals for the final treaty on wildlife management. Within this working group, mutual respect and understanding overcame the initial differences between traditional and non-traditional approaches to wildlife issues.

In the Sandspit harbour case, disagreement about the ecology of Brant geese led to the formation of a working group to develop a common assessment of what was known about local waterfowl ecology. The one-on-one format enabled both sides to step back, cool off, and reflect together on why the issue had become so adversarial. The exercise enabled parties to recast the issues in a more constructive way and to avoid personal recriminations. This positive experience had long-

lasting effects: months after the consensus process finished, the government representative continued to enjoy open discussions with the community on difficult issues. Such discussions would have been unthinkable prior to the working group experience.

Working groups can contribute significantly to building an agreement. Just as importantly, they help foster positive personal working relationships. A sense of cooperative teamwork is especially likely to emerge when small groups are mandated to explore and develop options that benefit all parties. The respect and understanding that develop within the working group can easily spread to others within the process.

## Informal contacts to promote greater understanding

Overcoming biases and stereotypes takes time and the opportunity to mingle not just as negotiators but as people. Informal contacts outside the more formal setting of the main negotiating table contribute greatly to building understanding, respect, and overall good working relationships.

Resolving issues within the Yukon land claims owed a great deal to informal contacts. Parties met during many informal occasions at kitchen or coffee tables, on city or country walks, in restaurants, or at fishing or hunting camps. Whether or not conversations eventually turned to the substance of land claims, these times were an integral part of the negotiation process.

The importance of informal exchanges is too often overlooked in designing a negotiating timetable. Ample time must be allowed for informal interaction, and some informal activities should be specifically planned. For example, workshops and working groups give parties a chance to interact casually. Other activities that promote informal interaction include

- joint field trips to the site of the conflict or to places where issues similar to those under discussion have been resolved,
- arranging lunch or dinner speakers on key topics,
- retreats to work on issues, with ample time allowed for socializing,
- opportunities to celebrate special occasions or join in activities, e.g., fishing trips, poker games, barbecues, golf tournaments, and so forth.

### Using skilled mediators to help with difficult issues

Skilled mediators are particularly valuable in negotiations involving parties with significantly different cultural backgrounds or values. While helping to manage the process in many other ways, these neutrals can play a vital bridging role when initial differences block effective communication.

Undisclosed assumptions about other parties' values, interests, and beliefs can become extremely destructive. Mediators, through private sessions with each party, can unearth inaccurate and exaggerated beliefs. They can also explore each party's private concerns about the other parties and about the negotiations. Using these insights, a neutral may be able to moderate the extreme views that parties may have about each other.

## The moderating influence of a mediator

The moderating influence of a mediator can also come into play in direct meetings among the parties. When tempers flare, a mediator can often intervene with skilful rephrasing of aggressive dialogue or by using the guidelines established by the parties to steer the process through difficult moments. This can defuse confrontation and — equally important in terms of this chapter — it can serve as a model for difficult but respectful exchanges. Parties begin to see how effective "empathic" communication can be and begin to practise more constructive approaches themselves.

Reinterpreting dialogue can help each party to see that a misunderstanding may have arisen more from lack of knowledge than from disrespect. A government or corporate suggestion to meet on a culturally important date may be innocent, but can be read as just another insult to a group's culture. So many process decisions must be made almost every day in negotiations that parties lacking a keen understanding of others' values, circumstances, and culture may inadvertently diminish the stock of goodwill within negotiations. Skilled neutrals have the time and the experience to reassure offended parties that mistakes are unintentional. They can also advise parties privately on how to avoid repeating such mistakes.

Skilled mediators acting as facilitators or keepers of the process can help prevent process or procedural difficulties that can block progress on substantive issues. The use of skilled mediators in large plenary sessions or in small working groups helps avoid breakdowns of respect or understanding that can be unnecessarily disruptive.

# Conclusion

This chapter has argued that negotiations are more effective if parties take time to appreciate one another's cultures, values, and circumstances. Agreements reached this way are more likely to survive the difficulties of ratification and implementation. Moreover, parties sacrifice none of their own interests or values in developing mutual respect and understanding.

A consensus process does not try to shape a settlement by eliminating value differences among the parties. Rather, by encouraging respect for and understanding of differences, it enables these differences to contribute to rather than hinder an agreement. Even if no agreement emerges, a process built upon mutual respect and understanding leaves vastly improved working relationships among the parties, which on another day may lead to an agreement.

When diversity is not respected, time and effort are often wasted on bitter and destructive disputes that threaten collective well-being. But when it is respected, diversity among parties can help forge the creative solutions required to develop and sustain healthy relationships and communities.

# Chapter 8
# Achieving Accountability in Consensus Processes

## Principle 8: Accountability

**The parties are accountable both to their constituencies and to the process that they have agreed to establish.**

"It is important that the participants representing groups or organizations effectively speak for the interests they represent. Mechanisms and resources for timely feedback and reporting to constituencies are crucial and need to be established. This builds understanding and commitment among the constituencies and minimizes surprises.

Given significant public concern about environmental, social, and economic issues, keeping the public informed on the development and outcome of any process is important."

— *Building Consensus for a Sustainable Future: Guiding Principles*

Consensus processes for public decision making give stakeholders more direct control over the quality and detail of decisions than do conventional decision-making processes. However, most people who will be affected by the outcome will not actually be negotiating. They must rely on their representatives to keep them informed of progress and involved in the process. Accountability thus becomes a key factor in the success of a consensus process.

To be accountable is to be answerable to someone for decisions and actions. It means not being able to say yes or no to terms of an agreement without taking account of how acceptable that deal may be to others. It is about having to explain actions or proposed actions and obtain approval for these.

This chapter begins by looking at the various "lines" of accountability that exist within consensus processes. It then focuses on the negotiator as representative, reviewing why it is so important for those at the table to establish and maintain an accountable relationship with constituents. It describes what representatives are accountable for — their duties on behalf of constituents — and outlines how accountability differs among organizations and groups. The chapter concludes with a review of the strategies and techniques that help develop accountability within consensus processes.

## Who is accountable and to whom?

The primary line of accountability is that between representatives and their constituencies. But there are other obligations involved.

## What is entailed in each of these lines of accountability?

### Negotiators to constituencies

As noted, the primary responsibility of negotiators is to their own constituency. Without the earned respect and confidence of those who are being represented, the negotiator has no authority or ability to develop an agreement with other groups. Less often mentioned is the two-way nature of this relationship. The constituency must also take responsibility for ensuring that representatives understand their mandate — and its limits. The constituency should also strive to "be there" for negotiators when they need feedback on key aspects of an emerging agreement: it is not unusual for representatives — especially those from middle levels of large organizations — to have difficulty getting the attention of senior decision makers. Senior decision makers must help negotiators to be accountable by setting aside the time for briefings and instruction; they must be committed to and supportive of the process.

### Negotiators to other negotiators

Negotiators must also be accountable to each other. When they are not — and undertakings or negotiated assurances are not honoured — stalemate and process breakdown inevitably follow. Chapter 4 stressed the significance of ground rules freely devised and committed to by all negotiators. These commitments can spell out how negotiators must act accountably with each other. Repeated violations of ground rules erode the trust and confidence essential in reaching agreement.

### Negotiators to authorities and stakeholders not at the table

Negotiators may also have to maintain at least an informal line of accountability to important groups who are not at the table. In some settings, the mere existence of a consensus process may be "at the pleasure" of those who make the final decisions. In the Sandspit harbour case, the federal minister of the environment had sanctioned use of mediation, against the backdrop of anticipated formal adoption after new federal environmental assessment legislation. And in Ontario, several consensus processes surrounding proposed landfill facilities have been undertaken under the authority of environmental regulatory boards. Clearly, in such cases the negotiators must be accountable to those ultimate decision makers, at least in the sense of operating within their rules and time frames. Even when there is no ultimate decision maker, parties negotiating about issues that have broad social effects should work to keep stakeholders who are not at the table well informed.

### Negotiators to the public

The negotiator may also need to be accountable to broader, ill-defined interests that are difficult to represent or are hard to communicate with — future generations or the broad public who, although numerous individually, have only a small stake in decisions under negotiation. This kind of challenge is addressed later in this chapter.

### Negotiators to the process

The principle of accountability also includes the less tangible accountability of the negotiator to the consensus process. Negotiators must respect the core principles of consensus building and behave in a manner that upholds the integrity of the process. In a similar way, lawyers pledge to act in a manner that preserves the traditions and values of the judicial process. Public acceptance of consensus processes will be compromised if negotiators bend rules and definitions capriciously, such as when negotiators pressure minorities who hold out against an emerging consensus, or when majority parties decide in frustration to accept less than unanimity as "virtual consensus." When this happens, the process loses credibility and, as one discouraged participant put it, becomes little more than "genteel bullying."

## How can a representative have room to negotiate and yet remain accountable to constituents?

At the table, especially in sustainability issues, discussions are complex and often highly technical. It is important for problem solving to proceed without frequent interruptions that break the flow. But how far can negotiators go in pursuing new directions without checking back with constituents? To pursue a novel resolution too far without some form of checking back is to risk isolation from those one represents and ultimate rejection of the resulting consensus.

Sometimes negotiators are relatively free to pursue a deal with other parties. They have the authority to work through proposals and counterproposals to the point of draft agreement. Only at that point must they seek ratification from constituents. This parallels the common system of elected representation used at all levels of government in Canada. Such a trustee system contrasts with representation by delegates.[12] In the most extreme version of the latter, the negotiator does little more than carry messages between the constituency and the bargaining table. In most consensus building, representatives have neither the full authority of a trustee nor the messenger role of a delegate. Each representative must deal with a tangle of seemingly contradictory forces when it comes to maintaining accountability at the table and at home.

## How do constituencies differ in the accountability required of their representatives?

Different types of stakeholders require different degrees of accountability from their representatives. This variation is reflected in group structure and internal communications. In some organizations, typically those using top-down decision making, the negotiator may have the authority to work out a deal, reporting back only infrequently through a well-defined chain of authority.

Often, company representatives whose experience of negotiations is based on collective bargaining between management and labour unions believe this structure should apply to consensus building for sustainability. But what if one or more of the organizations at the table makes its decisions solely by internal consensus, taking each member's views equally into account before finalizing any collective position?

For many First Nations this structure, rather than a hierarchy, captures the essence of internal organization. Other groups may have quite different decision-making structures. For example, rarely will federal or provincial government departments be represented by

the highest (i.e., ministerial or deputy-ministerial) levels. Negotiators may be mid-level officials who face elaborate and time-consuming procedures to get formal approval of developments in the negotiations.

Non-government organizations (NGOs) vary widely in internal structure. Many try to be consensus-based. In practice, however, the system of representation may be nebulous at best. Some members may believe that the representative has the authority to work out a deal while others demand more of a delegate reporting system. Such uncertainty may make accountability far more complicated for an NGO representative than for some other negotiators.

At such a table, there is a high potential for misunderstanding and resentment due to different reporting requirements. For the hierarchically structured company, approval for new ideas contributing to a resolution, if required at all, may be one phone call away. The government representative may need much more time to seek approvals up the organizational ladder. The First Nation representative will often insist on checking significant new directions with the entire community through traditional consensus procedures. And the NGO spokesperson may have to grope for organizational support amid a bewildering array of divergent internal perspectives.

Such diverse requirements can be frustrating but are manageable, provided that a candid and sincere effort is made early in the process to clarify each representative's organizational culture. Recognizing the special challenges that each representative faces in being accountable becomes part of the larger effort of developing rapport and respect (see Chapter 7).

## What strategies and techniques help in achieving accountability?

### Negotiators to constituencies

How does a negotiator account to those represented? There are basically two related tasks to accomplish in maintaining accountability: the first is to keep the people who are represented well informed about developments at the table. The second is to obtain their approval for commitments. Work on both these tasks must go on throughout the consensus process: rarely can a representative wait until a settlement is practically final before informing and seeking advice from constituents.

The diverse groups participating in sustainability discussions will have different reporting requirements. For organizations with well-established communication channels and hierarchical structures, the negotiating representative may only have to circulate occasional memos to update colleagues or report orally during regular meetings. Within First Nations, there may be time-honoured but very different means of communicating and deciding consensually: special meetings may have to be called at critical points in negotiations, both for briefing the community and for gauging support.

In other groups, especially NGOs that may have come together only when the issue being negotiated arose, the representative may need to report back more often. During the Sandspit harbour mediation, the environmental coalition, formed as the process began, received both written and oral reports after each negotiating session. Sandspit community representatives relied on regular community meetings, especially at points when

negotiations took a new turn. For example, when site relocation became a strong possibility, a special meeting was called to inform the new neighbours of one of the leading potential sites.

The mechanisms for maintaining the communications essential for accountability vary among groups. At the outset of negotiations, representatives must try to make clear to other representatives exactly what time and resources they will need for briefing their constituents. This will help allay suspicions about intentional stalling and game playing later on.

Whatever the reporting needs of groups, some tools are generally useful for enhancing communications between representatives and constituencies during consensus processes. The negotiating group can record and circulate meeting notes. Often, consensus processes rely on concise records of meetings that summarize the general nature and direction of discussions without specifying who said what. This format can convey a sense of what is happening without inhibiting free discussion by the negotiators. Meeting notes can be sent directly to the full membership of small NGOs, placed in libraries or other public places, regularly inserted in local newspapers either as paid advertising or columns, and circulated as memos within government agencies or corporations.

A mediator may also play an important role in helping negotiators maintain accountability with constituents. During the Sandspit harbour process, the mediator joined different representatives in constituency briefings — the small group sessions of the environmentalists, the community-wide meetings of the village of Sandspit, and the "boardrooms" of several government agencies.

This meant that the representative was not alone nor taking the lead in explaining the negotiating stance of opponents.

As noted, accountability requires gauging constituency support for an emerging consensus. Some of the tools used in putting out information may also help in testing the acceptability of an agreement or its particular elements. Long before a final settlement is considered, representatives will generally want to seek constituents' opinions about tentative agreements. This can be done through informal one-on-one discussions or by using well-established techniques for surveying public preferences. These can range from detailed opinion surveys to advisory referenda.

Toward the end of the Sandspit harbour mediation, professionally designed "open houses" were held to enable extensive small group and one-on-one discussions of details of the proposed settlement and an "exit survey." This gave local representatives and others at the table a better sense of how local people viewed the alternatives that were eventually incorporated into the consensus plan. A second round of open houses provided a final opportunity to gauge public reaction and gave the negotiating team a chance to explain publicly why a decision had been made. This frequently neglected component of accountability includes explicit responses to objections from individuals who continue to reject the negotiated outcome.

### Negotiators to other negotiators

The first responsibility of negotiators is to their constituents; however, they are also accountable to one another. These responsibilities can conflict, and negotiators may be tempted to play these responsibilities off against each other. How far should a representative go in urging constituents to accept a settlement that he or she feels is as good as can be achieved? To what extent should he or she use the reluctance of constituents to endorse an agreement as a way to gain more concessions from other parties?

It is easy for negotiators to end up manipulating rather than dealing straightforwardly with constituents and other negotiators. The best solution may be for negotiators to distinguish clearly between firm commitments and possibilities requiring further consideration and consultation with constituents. There are several ways of doing this. It may be useful to identify stages when there can be "invention without commitment." Innovative ideas can flow freely without anyone having to check back with constituents, and ideas that seem worthwhile can be brought back to constituents as needed. It may also help if negotiators can assure one another and constituents that all agreements on individual issues remain tentative until a total package, wholly acceptable to all parties, is produced.

### Negotiators to authorities and stakeholders not at the table

Chapter 2 suggested that, in addition to stakeholders who are represented in negotiations, there are likely to be others who are either directly affected or have a key role to play in implementation. The key to accountability with such groups is information — keeping them informed of the course of negotiations. The tools for communicating with constituencies may also be useful here: for example, regular meeting notes or special sessions to explain what is happening at the table. In the Sandspit harbour case, the mediator was directed to ensure information flowed to the Council of the Haida Nation, which had chosen not to participate directly. Meeting notes and update memos were provided throughout the negotiations. Toward the end of the process, a special joint session was arranged with Council representatives and the whole negotiating team. This provided an opportunity to ensure that the emerging consensus was acceptable to the Haida leadership.

The same approach can be used to inform key regulatory agencies about a draft agreement and gauge attitudes toward it. In the Sandspit case, federal environmental officials who were responsible for dredging and dredge spoil disposal were invited to a regular meeting to exchange information on their requirements and on technical aspects of the draft settlement. These kinds of interactions are key to achieving some degree of accountability with key stakeholders and authorities that are not at the negotiating table.

### Negotiators to the public

The increasing use of consensus processes has led to questions about how the public interest, broadly speaking, is to be protected. What is the public interest? One view is that the public interest is simply the sum of the many individual special interests in society, in which case it is protected simply by ensuring the right mix and diversity of participants at the consensus table. Another view is that elected politicians are the best arbiters of this broader interest. According to this view, their presence at the table would solve the problem of accountability. If that is not possible, their

duly appointed officials can stand in and thereby defend the public interest.

There is no simple solution to the challenge of protecting the public interest. But there are several safeguards against the worst-case fear that consensus processes are nothing more than a handful of special interests cutting deals in their own favour. One of the most important safeguards is to maintain as much as possible an open and visible process. This is not always easy: negotiators often need (or feel they need) privacy —especially during sensitive bargaining when tentative ideas on trade-offs need to be tested.

When sessions are closed, it is all the more important to provide a candid explanation of progress in the process and to distribute information promptly. In this regard, it can be very useful to meet with the media to indicate when and how information will be made available. Some negotiating groups include such protocols within their process ground rules. By working closely with the media, participants in consensus processes can help prevent the impression that special interests are being favoured behind closed doors.

Linking consensus processes to more familiar legal and political institutions is another important way of improving public confidence and accountability. An interesting example comes from Quebec. There, a quasi-judicial agency, the Bureau d'audiences publiques sur l'environnement (BAPE), has developed a strong mediating role based on its authority to investigate the environmental effects of provincial government undertakings. Instead of simply holding hearings, BAPE brings parties together to seek common ground for a settlement. Mediation is becoming an institution within environmental assessment processes elsewhere across Canada. Wedding ad hoc consensus processes to existing and recognized means of environmental review is an important way of protecting — and being seen to protect — the broader public interest.

### Negotiators to the process

As noted earlier, negotiators need to be accountable to the process itself in much the same way that lawyers need to be accountable to the legal process. This accountability is accomplished by fully observing the other forms of accountability outlined here. If those at the table maintain good working relationships with their constituents, with each other, and with those not at the table, they will advance public confidence in and respect for consensus processes.

## Accountability and the mediator

Mediators are increasingly being used to help groups resolve disputes over sustainability issues. The question naturally arises of how and in what ways these "helpers" can be held accountable. Further, how can mediators help those at the table to be good representatives for their own constituencies?

The mediator must be primarily accountable to the negotiators but, arguably, may also have responsibilities in terms of external regulatory agencies, politicians, and even perhaps to the "public interest" and unrepresented groups. Trade-offs may be involved when the question arises: is the mediator there to help parties achieve a just settlement — or just a settlement?

Professionals in the field of dispute resolution hold different views about the nature of mediator accountability. Some feel that the mediator is solely answerable to the parties at the table: if the parties reach an agreement, the mediator's job is complete. Others feel that the mediator should be aware of unrepresented interests (including the public interest) and should take some responsibility for making sure weaker parties get to and are effective at the bargaining table.

Mediators should probably opt for a fairly conservative role, since they must ultimately defer to the wishes of parties at the table. Moreover, to assume responsibility for the welfare of the underprivileged and voiceless is beyond their professional competence. However, mediators should be able to point out when, in their judgement, emerging consensus agreements fail to take account of interests beyond the bargaining table. It is precisely because mediators are servants of the process that they are obliged to speak up when disregarding interests not at the table could jeopardize prospective outcomes.

A mediator can also help negotiators with their own issues of accountability, by assisting representatives at constituency briefing sessions, coordinating the provision of public information, and liaising with key parties who are not at the table. Often a mediator can carry difficult messages, playing the "agent of reality" in briefing both constituencies and key decision makers. When the Alberta-Pacific negotiations almost broke down over one government agency's wish to revise what other parties thought was a final agreement, the mediator worked with senior officials to help them rethink their agency's insistence on the revisions. Because he could go to the top without having to work through the "proper channels," the mediator was able to help the parties find a quick and reasonable solution for a problem threatening the entire process.

Broadly speaking, a mediator's most important contribution may be to keep issues of accountability in front of negotiators. Disputes over sustainability can be very complex. Immersed in detail, representatives can lose sight of constituency views and needs. Mediators can keep probing the representatives on the extent of their constituents' understanding and support for the direction negotiations are taking. This will remind each negotiator to brief and obtain guidance or approval from constituents.

## Conclusion

This chapter has emphasized how dependent "doing the right thing" is on context, especially on the different organizational and cultural settings of the various parties. These differences and their implications for the accountability of each representative need to be fully understood as early as possible in the process.

A negotiator has a special responsibility to make other participants aware of the difficult issues that he or she will face. Some ground rules specify the responsibility of each negotiator to flag difficult issues so that other negotiators are clear about the internal positions and demands of a party. When negotiators gloss over these difficulties, other parties get a false sense of progress. Effective negotiators say something like, "I might be able to live with that personally, but I could never get support from my organization. They are going to raise the following questions and objections...." In this way, key problems are stated, but the opposition does not appear personal.

The position of a negotiator in a consensus process involving diverse organizations is inherently difficult and personally challenging. Through careful preparation and continuing vigilance, negotiators can be accountable as representatives working between their constituency and the consensus-building process.

# Chapter 9
# Setting Time Limits in Consensus Processes

## PRINCIPLE 9: Time Limits

### Realistic deadlines are necessary throughout the process.

"Clear and reasonable time limits for working toward a conclusion and reporting on results should be established. Such milestones bring focus to the process, marshal key resources, and mark progress toward consensus.

Sufficient flexibility, however, is necessary to embrace shifts or changes in timing."

— *Building Consensus for a Sustainable Future: Guiding Principles*

An attractive feature of consensus is the opportunity it offers to settle differences among parties in a timely manner. Often, adversaries turn to direct negotiations to settle disputes that have lasted years, or because of the prospect of lengthy administrative hearings or trials in court.

This chapter examines the challenges that time and timeliness pose for any group operating by consensus. It begins by reviewing why consensus groups should have time limits and what events or considerations can put a time limit on the process. It shows how time limits can give structure and focus to the entire process and explains why consensus groups should be flexible and realistic about deadlines. The chapter concludes by summarizing several strategies to assist groups in making time limits a key asset in successful consensus processes.

## Why should consensus groups have time limits?

> *Depend on it, Sir, when a man knows he is to be hanged in a fortnight,*
> *it concentrates his mind wonderfully.*
> — Samuel Johnson

Setting and observing time limits helps consensus groups in several important ways. As noted, face-to-face negotiations are often the last resort of parties who have been frustrated by a long and expensive struggle. They need strong incentives to start and to stay with a demanding consensus process (see Chapter 1). By setting time limits at the outset, participants reassure each other of their commitment to reach closure.

Often, parties' interests are affected quite differently by the passage of time. Proponents of

development may desperately want to get started, while others may welcome delay. In these cases and others, it is important to have a schedule that confirms the unanimous intent of all parties to work together toward agreement.

In dealing with sustainability issues, the representatives at the negotiating table are not alone in seeking a timely conclusion. The welfare and peace of mind of many other people — notably representatives' constituents and decision makers — are also at stake. Those who are not at the table can find it difficult to see why the process takes so long — after all, they are not privy to the intricacies of the issues nor can they really appreciate, as representatives do, how time consuming it can be to establish trust and a constructive working relationship. Clear, credible, and public deadlines reassure constituents and the broader community of the seriousness and diligence of the negotiators.

Another reason for establishing deadlines is the "pet topic" pitfall. All the parties may agree that timely resolution is essential in principle. But each will want to spend endless time analysing, reflecting on, and deliberating over certain special issues. In the Sandspit harbour mediation, supporters never tired of explaining how the project would redress the economic hardships faced by their community. Environmental advocates had limited interest in this topic but would gladly engage in extensive discussions of waterfowl. Without a "negotiated" sense of urgency, reflected in agreed-upon deadlines, each party's focus on their priority topics could have drawn out the process significantly.

As the process concludes, the existence of a time limit may help representatives explain proposed accommodations and "packages" taking shape to their constituents. Groups represented in negotiations will always wonder whether their spokesperson could have done better. The knowledge that representatives achieved an acceptable deal within a reasonable but firm deadline can help constituents understand why a proposed agreement, as the Sandspit mediation team concluded in its final report, "is not necessarily optimal from the perspective of any particular party, but from the perspective of the mediation team as a whole, it represents the consensus achieved, taking into account the diverse and often competing interests and values around the Table."

Time limits can also be useful in the form of milestones throughout the process. Working from a realistic overall deadline, consensus groups can work backwards to develop a credible plan of achievements for the entire process. These milestones help give the negotiating group a sense of accomplishment during those long weeks or months of discussion when prospects for a conclusive settlement can seem remote.

## Where do time limits come from?

Time limits can arise from several different considerations. First, there are deadlines over which there is no human control. For example, in recent years fisheries agencies have relied increasingly on stakeholder negotiations to plan annual harvests of fish stocks. Many species are migratory and their movements define the schedule that fishers must follow to ensure a successful harvest. Likewise, negotiations among different fishing sectors — sport, commercial, and Aboriginal fishers — are tightly constrained by nature itself. Fishing

plans prepared after a salmon run has passed by are irrelevant.

Other factors defining the time available for consensus building may be of human origin. A regulatory commission or review board may be required by law to make its decision within a fixed period. If a consensus process is within the purview of such a board, there may be no way to extend the deadline. If the negotiating group knows this from the outset and has organized itself accordingly, an inflexible deadline can be an asset. In Peterborough, Ontario, a regulatory board reviewing an application for an extension to a landfill passed its time limits on to a multi-party group established to negotiate permit conditions. With the clear understanding of how little time was available, the negotiating team was able to get organized and reach consensus on all issues by the deadline.

Sometimes an impending election may provide a powerful incentive for parties to reach agreement. For projects with a high political profile, the prospect of having to deal with a new elected representative, council, minister, or government may be a powerful motivator. In the Sandspit harbour case, the negotiating team was very conscious of an imminent federal election that could bring in new cabinet ministers unfamiliar with the federal government's original commitment to the project.[13] This prospect helped bring discussions to a close. In the Ontario mercury pollution settlement, the key factor in the timing of the ratification process and final voting by the White Dog community was the imminence of a band election.

Other external time limits may be arbitrarily imposed. For example, an ultimate decision maker may set a completion date to keep the consensus group working hard. When a decision maker decides to do this, he or she must be fully aware of both the generic challenges in any consensus process and the specific challenges of the case at hand. An arbitrary deadline set without appreciation for the real difficulties of building trust, sharing information, bargaining, getting constituency support, and so forth is doomed to lead to failure and thereby undermine public support for consensus building.

Parties considering the use of consensus should think hard about what is really involved, preferably with advice from process managers or others who have been through such processes. They should not hesitate to inform ultimate decision makers if imposed time limits seem unreasonable.

Some consensus groups may have no externally imposed deadline. Their deadlines arise through early, open, and, if needed, repeated discussion of time limits within the consensus team. Like external decision makers, the team may wish to set an arbitrary deadline based on informed hunches by people with experience in consensus building. The understanding can be that they will try to finish by that date. If they cannot, they will use the occasion for critical assessment of progress.

Another approach is to set a deadline acceptable to the most anxious participant on the understanding that it may be hard to achieve. The consensus team can commit to a good faith effort to meet the deadline but also agree that at this date they will assess progress. It can be further agreed that parties who feel headway is insufficient at that point may reconsider their involvement in the process. This approach can reassure more anxious parties while encouraging others to avoid delays.

## How long does a consensus process take?

The duration of consensus processes varies enormously, affected by the number of parties involved, by the range and complexity of issues under consideration, and by a host of external developments that can change the dynamics of the process and even the issues under discussion. This makes it very difficult, at the outset, to estimate the time required.

A consensus process on sustainability issues typically requires many months. In the Sandspit harbour mediation, it took four months to identify all key interests and for all parties to obtain required permissions to come to the table. Another month passed in selecting a mediator. Five months had elapsed before discussions could even begin.

At the first meeting in April 1992, supporters of the harbour development raised concern over the suggested three-month deadline for completing discussions. Recalling their experience with time-consuming labour-management negotiations and anxious to proceed in light of delays already experienced, they pushed for an even shorter time frame. Other parties recognized the complexity of the issues and eventually secured agreement for a three-month deadline, after which progress would be reviewed.

This deadline passed with agreement nowhere in sight. But all parties were better informed and appreciated the challenges involved in systematically reviewing and agreeing on the many issues. To make the process more efficient, working groups were formed to grapple with specific topics ranging from wildlife ecology to the socio-economic implications of alternative harbour sites. Some further baseline technical information needs were then identified. Six months had passed since the first meeting.

Subsequently, as the mediation team began to look at previously unconsidered harbour locations, new parties emerged whose interests could be affected by developments in these locations. The mediation team expanded and made an even greater effort to get information out to the public. New technical issues were raised by the consideration of alternative sites. Only after eight months of intensive effort was a draft agreement-in-principle tabled. Then all the representatives had to review the agreement with constituencies. Additional issues were raised that had to be dealt with. Because of the complexity of the ecological and engineering issues, the mediation team decided to hold a full "open house." Following this, they met to consider public feedback and once again refine the plan.

Then some limited but vocal opposition began to organize against the recommended and widely reviewed harbour site. Another series of open houses was held so that misunderstandings could be cleared up and community opinion gauged. When these were completed, a final report was signed. The date was June 11, 1993, 14 months after the first meeting.

During the consensus process, the "final" deadline had come around several times and, after careful review of problems and accomplishments, been extended. The Sandspit case illustrates two general and important points about the expected duration of a consensus process: first, it is very difficult to foresee all the factors influencing the time horizon during the process. Second, in light of this uncertainty, it is important to have real deadlines accompanied by an understanding that

if time runs out, the parties will discuss progress and the significance of the delay. By talking openly about difficulties, the consensus group reduces suspicions of intentional stalling and develops a better appreciation for the complexities of their common challenge.

## How can time limits help structure a consensus process?

Setting deadlines is more than simply agreeing on a final date by which consensus must be reached: when groups take time limits seriously, they begin to see consensus building for the complex project it is. If an end date has been set, however tentatively, questions follow about tasks that must be completed, how these relate to each other, and who is going to do them and when. When someone calls for better information on some controversial matter, questions arise about whether it is available within the time frame, how it can be obtained most efficiently, and whether a longer time frame should be set. And so on. The point is that when a consensus group operates within an agreed time frame, it plans its work in more detail than if no deadline existed. It develops a more comprehensive sense of the steps and tasks essential to consensus building and of the collective resources of the group. What was an adversarial collection of negotiators develops some of the features of a project planning team.

## Why do time limits need to be realistic and flexible?

Time limits must be realistic in the sense of being achievable in light of the work facing the consensus group. Sometimes a deadline is so tight that following the other equally important guiding principles covered in this book becomes impossible. For example, the principle of self-design (see Chapter 4) says the parties need to establish their own fully acceptable ground rules. This takes time. Yet, often when representatives first meet they begin negotiating without detailed consideration of procedural matters. The result is almost certain to be confusion and delay later on as parties wrangle over process.

Similarly, a rush to make progress in negotiations can reduce accountability to those not at the table (see Chapter 8). This is likely to undermine any proposed settlement, as it did in a consensus process dealing with liability issues for contaminated sites. In 1992, the Canadian Council of Ministers of the Environment (CCME) established a core group, operating by consensus, to develop proposals on this complex matter and to present them to the next full CCME meeting. Shortly before that meeting, several core group members encountered opposition to the proposals within their constituent organizations. A hard deadline had prevented the dialogue necessary to explain the draft proposals to constituents and to accommodate their concerns.

Time limits for consensus building need to allow for some flexibility to accommodate unexpected changes (see Chapter 5). Even in engineering projects, planners always provide leeway for unanticipated events that lengthen the time required for completion. The need for contingency planning is that much greater in consensus building, where so much depends on human understanding, learning, and reactions to new situations. A consensus process entails a wide array of tasks, each of which may produce surprises, sometimes because of developments within the process, sometimes

because of outside factors beyond the parties' control.

Time limits also need to be flexible to allow for the differing ways parties deal with deadlines and their differing abilities to commit to a fixed schedule for securing constituency support. Such differences are particularly evident in the many Canadian environmental struggles where Aboriginal peoples play a leading role. The requirement to meet firm deadlines may become quite inappropriate — and unproductive — as cultural factors come into play.

For example, in one consensus-building process on resources co-management in British Columbia, government officials pressed for a fixed and quite tight deadline. An Aboriginal representative countered with a very pointed question: how, he asked, did government think they would solve a problem in a month or two that had taken more than a century to create? Many of the generalities about time and its management, which non-Aboriginals see as given, are foreign to Aboriginal culture. Traditional indigenous communities see human projects as subject to natural rhythms and vulnerable to the unforeseen. Limiting a consensus process to hard and fast deadlines may seem as absurd as expecting wild animals to appear at a set time for hunters.

First Nation representatives, as well as representatives of non-governmental organizations, may have more difficulty than other participants in predicting the time needed to discuss consensus proposals with their constituencies. In a hierarchically organized corporation, a spokesperson usually knows when senior staff will finish reviewing a draft consensus document. In government agencies, especially where ministerial approval is needed, scheduling is less predictable. For Aboriginal peoples, whose decisions are often made through community discussions on which no time limits are acceptable, firm commitments to a ratification deadline may be difficult. All groups need to understand the "political cultures" of the groups with whom they negotiate.

This is not to say that time limits are impossible to set in cross-cultural contexts. But, as with all elements of process design, early consideration, sensitive and respectful discussion, openness to alternatives, and an unshakable commitment to satisfying all parties are essential.

## Balancing flexibility and the benefits of time limits

This chapter has outlined two seemingly contradictory ideas about time limits: on the one hand, firm deadlines provide clear benefits in providing incentives, maintaining credibility and enthusiasm, and helping parties to share and allocate their resources to get tasks done on time. On the other hand, time limits must be adjustable to ensure that the process follows other guiding principles, allows for the unexpected, and is open to cultural and related differences among the parties. How can consensus groups set time limits that are both firm and flexible? Three strategies can help consensus groups in this.

### 1. Take deadlines seriously but use them also as opportunities for assessment and learning

Respect for time limits is not an either/or choice. Groups can agree in good faith to strive for completion of particular tasks or overall consensus within a set time frame. But they also should recognize explicitly from the

outset of negotiations that unforeseeable events can occur. A missed deadline should be seen as an opportunity for groups to diagnose their difficulties, pinpoint sources of delay, and determine whether they can do things differently and better. It is important to clarify whether a deadline was missed because some party failed in its commitments (and, if so, why) or whether the cause was beyond the membership's control. Parties may conclude they are spending too much time on activities that are not essential. In the early months of the Sandspit harbour process, the mediation group frequently sought new technical information. But as time — and deadlines— passed, they became more selective in deciding what information was really needed. Review of the reasons for early delays helped discipline their process.

### 2. Use interim milestones

While the purpose of negotiations is to achieve a final consensus, interim tasks can appropriately be scheduled as milestones for consensus building. The following activities are common to most consensus processes and can serve this purpose:

- agreement on written ground rules,
- inventory, compilation, and circulation to all parties of a full set of relevant technical information and background documents,
- reports from subcommittees and working groups to the full consensus team,
- completion of a first working draft of an agreement package, and
- completion of consultations with constituencies.

Each of these or other appropriately chosen milestones afford the group two significant opportunities: first, when setting a time line, all parties come to a better and shared understanding of key steps in the consensus process; second, when a deadline is reached, the group will have valuable feedback on its collective ability to perform important tasks.

### 3. Talk about time from the outset

Consensus groups must take the time to talk about time, right from the beginning of the process. Missed deadlines can heighten mistrust and lead to accusations of stalling and bad faith. Or, they can be opportunities for everyone to better grasp the difficulties inherent in collaborative problem solving. Whether time limits have positive or negative effects depends on dialogue. An appreciation for this point and regular discussion of progress and problems improves the chances of a successful — and timely — consensus.

## Conclusion

Representatives in a consensus process can easily be overwhelmed as they work to resolve an enormous array of issues as well as keep constituents informed of progress. Early in the process, however, they must give serious consideration to time limits; if they do not, they may jeopardize good working relationships with constituents and the process itself. By setting reasonable deadlines, gauging progress, and revising time lines only as needed, representatives can help maintain mutual trust, momentum, and public support throughout the process.

# Chapter 10
# Implementing Consensus Agreements

## PRINCIPLE 10: Implementation

**Commitments to implementation and effective monitoring are essential parts of any agreement.**

"Parties must be satisfied that their agreements will be implemented. As a result, all parties should discuss the goals of the process and how results will be handled. Clarifying a commitment to implementing the outcome of the process is essential.

The support and commitment of any party responsible for follow-up is critical. When decisions require government action, the participation of government authorities from the outset is crucial.

A post-agreement mechanism should be established to monitor implementation and deal with problems that may arise."

— *Building Consensus for a Sustainable Future: Guiding Principles*

The shift to consensus-based multistakeholder decision making requires paying much more attention to implementation — to turning all the good talk into action. This chapter addresses the challenge of implementation. It begins by underlining the importance of planning for implementation throughout a consensus process. Next it probes why implementation is often neglected despite its critical importance. How can parties who invest so much time and organizational resources in negotiations overlook the need to develop ways to bring it to life? Finally, this chapter discusses what an implementation plan must contain to help the agreement survive in the post-negotiation, unpredictable world, and outlines some strategies to support this last but perhaps most important enduring principle of consensus building.

## Why is focusing on implementation so important in consensus processes?

Legislatures and courts have the clearly defined resources (funds, staff, and coercive power) needed to ensure compliance and implementation. In contrast, the majority of consensus processes used to settle sustainability issues take place in much less structured, more uncertain circumstances. The need to focus on and plan the details of implementation is therefore much greater than in conventional decision-making forums.

A focus on implementation throughout a consensus process improves the quality and efficiency of discussions. Problem-solving groups can yield innovative but impractical ideas. Attention to how and whether particular suggestions could be implemented can save a group from wasting time and resources chasing impractical solutions.

Gaining an appreciation for how a possible solution can be implemented can also generate hope, even enthusiasm, for involvement in negotiations. Conversely, a failure to think through implementation can undo confidence and mutual trust in negotiations, when unrealistic "solutions" force negotiators to revisit old issues and redo work they thought was behind them. The following remarks from two long-term participants in the Yukon land claims show how thinking about implementation can generate enthusiasm for the difficult work of negotiating:

*When the talk turned to how it all might be done, you know, what was necessary for it all to work, then we began to imagine what it would look like. And for the first time, the very first time, I began to believe. You know, to believe that an agreement could actually one day happen. That was an important day for my commitment to the process.* — First Nation Representative

*Land claims had been just talk for over a dozen years — lots of people negotiating, nothing happening. I didn't support it because I knew it would never amount to more than talk. I changed my view right after they got me involved and the talk turned to how we might actually carry out the agreement. I would be involved with the parts that fell to my department to implement. That made me responsible to ensure the agreement could work; it gave me ownership in the success of the negotiation.* — Public Servant, Yukon Government

## Why do negotiators frequently avoid dealing with implementation?

Despite the benefits stemming from careful attention to implementation issues, parties often postpone or spend too little time working out how an agreement will be put into effect.

Implementation issues are often overlooked in the midst of the tremendous pressures on negotiators to reach an agreement. A crisis atmosphere encourages leaders to focus on finding rapid agreement on the most urgent issues; the less pressing work of determining how an agreement will be implemented is put off until some vague time in the future. Agreements reached this way tend to generate more problems than they solve. Often, the breakdown of a hastily conceived agreement diminishes the ability of parties to forge a later, lasting agreement.

As well, the challenges of implementation are often trivialized: many negotiators assume that once the "real" work of reaching an agreement is done, the purely technical and logistical issues will be readily resolved. Too often, negotiators rely on unrealistic assumptions about funding, regulatory approvals, and the cooperation of people and agencies who have not been involved in reaching the agreement.

Negotiators tend to see their responsibility solely in terms of "reaching" an agreement. Like runners in a relay race, negotiators too often pass the agreement, like a baton, to others to implement. This tendency can undermine the potential of any agreement to resolve differences or to be a viable and enduring solution.

Negotiators may also avoid implementation issues to create a "can do" atmosphere. People who ask: "But, what if...?" or "Yes, but how are we going to...?" are cast as nay sayers and as stifling essential creative problem solving. Group pressures to be positive can lead to "group think" whereby faulty solutions become the dubious foundation of an agreement, and the mechanics of making the agreement work are buried at the never-reached bottom of negotiating agendas.

Finally, inadequate attention to implementation can arise when negotiators do not have contact with those who will be needed to approve or implement the agreement. Often overlooked are the field or line staff whose understanding, compliance, and capability will be instrumental in successfully implementing the agreement. Also forgotten at key points are the senior officials and political leaders whose consent may ultimately be needed.

## What needs to be considered when planning for implementation?

Table 10-1 presents key questions that must be answered throughout implementation planning.

### Is the solution technically and legally sound?

Consensus processes dealing with environment and development issues often address complex matters that, in other forums, are relegated almost exclusively to experts. By being fully inclusive, the process necessarily involves representatives unevenly equipped to deal with technical assessments and legal issues. As consensus emerges on required actions, the parties will need to test the technical feasibility and legal dimensions of each part of the agreement. Legal limitations need to be identified, but care must be taken not to impede the creative problem solving

## Box 10-1

### Key Elements in Implementation Plans for Consensus Processes

| What to ask | What to do |
|---|---|
| Is the solution technically and legally sound? | Carry out technical and legal assessment of draft agreements (e.g., through expert review, role playing, simulated problem solving) |
| Will those whose support will be needed (i.e., constituents, politicians, other affected stakeholders) accept the agreement? | Regularly sound out constituents and other key parties, pre-implement selected aspects of agreement |
| How will formal ratification be achieved? | Clarify each party's ratification procedures |
| How will implementation be funded? | Identify funding sources |
| Who will be responsible for doing what? | Define roles/responsibilities |
| When will parts of the agreement be implemented? | Set schedules and priorities |
| Will actions follow agreed commitments? | Establish monitoring system |
| How will parties hold each other to commitments? | Create compliance measures |
| How will promises turn into action? | Negotiate action plan |
| What about unforeseen difficulties? | Develop contingency plans |

needed to overcome seemingly insurmountable impasses. Technical experts can assess the feasibility of new ideas. If challenged, many experts can open new avenues to solutions. In all instances where experts are called in, they should be accessible to all parties and, as much as possible, seen and used as neutral resources.

### Will those whose support will be needed accept the agreement?

If negotiators have maintained active contact with constituents (see Chapter 8), they will have a better idea of the acceptability, and therefore "implementability," of proposed agreements. Usually, some kind of "sign-off" or ratification will be required from several constituencies and external regulatory agencies. Implementation plans should specify how this will occur. As well, during implementation planning, ways can be developed to "pre-implement" part of the agreement to test its viability and assess its acceptability to all significant parties and constituencies ("pre-implementation" is discussed below).

### How will formal ratification be achieved?

Ratification requirements will differ among the parties. Each negotiator should set out how agreements will be ratified within his or her own constituency. A small organization may have only one or two levels of decision making, whereas a large organization such as a corporation or government body will have many.

In government agencies and corporations, authority tends to flow from the top down. This makes the giving and receiving of direction quite straightforward. In many non-governmental groups, authority tends to flow from the bottom up. First Nations, who traditionally operate by consensus, may need to hold extensive formal and informal meetings in their communities before ratification is assured. In some groups, ratification is further complicated by the need to maintain a working consensus, a particularly time-consuming and difficult exercise. Elected bodies such as legislatures or town councils operate from the top down but usually require a vote to conclude ratification. This can result in intense lobbying and delays in obtaining a decision. All parties need to be aware of and respect the ratification processes of others. Knowing what ratification steps are required early in the process avoids unrealistic expectations and suspicions about apparent delays in ratification. An implementation plan must be sensitive to the different pressures, time, and resources each party needs to ratify an agreement.

### How will implementation be funded?

All solutions cost something. An implementation plan must factor in not only original project costs but additional costs imposed by the agreement — for example, the costs of monitoring environmental effects — and who will pay. Where a consensus process creates a new policy, new funding questions will arise. If the agreement includes, for example, more extensive public scrutiny of annual cutting plans, will costs be paid by government, industry, or non-governmental groups? Misunderstandings over the source of funding are notoriously disruptive.

### Who will be responsible for doing what?

Each party's role in implementing an agreement should be specified. The resources each group needs to meet obligations should also be identified. Ascertaining the ability of each party to provide the resources to meet their commitments in a timely manner is essential. Confusion over the timing, funding, and nature of commitments can quickly rupture the threads binding parties to an agreement.

### When will parts of the agreement be implemented?

Chapter 9 stressed the importance of well-established time limits during the consensus process to maintain momentum and parties' trust in each other. The same holds true for implementation. Especially for agreements that contain many interdependent commitments, it is essential that parties know when and how various parts of the agreement will be implemented. Major difficulties arise when each party expects that elements of the agreement most important to them will be given priority. Consensus must be reached on realistic time limits, resource commitments, and obligations. Rarely should an implementation plan enable one party to receive all its benefits from an agreement before other parties begin to realize theirs.

*Will actions follow agreed commitments?*

Complex consensus agreements are neither self-executing nor self-enforcing. The implementation plan must contain a way of ensuring that commitments are being carried out according to the spirit and letter of consensus agreements. Monitoring gives parties early warning of implementation problems and of adjustments required to carry out the agreement effectively and economically. A good monitoring system can reassure parties that the objectives of the agreement are being realized and flag matters requiring remedial action or renegotiation.

*How will parties hold each other to commitments?*

Trust and good working relationships are built during negotiations. But, often, more than this is needed during implementation to convince constituencies and the general public that all parties will live up to their commitments. The stakes are often too high for those most affected by the agreement to take compliance as a given. Each party's interests are served when all parties confirm good will by binding themselves in some way to the agreement. Whether the means are legally based (e.g., formal contracts), financial (e.g., performance bonds), or otherwise, the implementation plan should stipulate how each signatory's obligations will be enforced.

*How will promises turn into action?*

Agreements may specify the range of actions that parties accept as a total package. But such a list is not a sufficient blueprint for implementation. All commitments in an agreement must be translated into a cohesive action plan. While parties do not need to spell out every step required to carry out an agreement, they should at least agree on a process that will settle what must be done at specified times. Overall, the action plan should provide all the answers to the questions discussed above.

*What strategies and techniques improve the likelihood of successful implementation?*

Consensus groups should carefully consider all issues that might arise in putting their agreement into effect. They should also consider what safety nets are necessary for their agreement to endure.

*Including the implementors*

Persons responsible for implementing an agreement must be highly motivated to invest the energy necessary to institute the changes called for by the agreement. An intolerant or apathetic attitude on the part of someone charged with implementation can undermine the prospects for timely and successful implementation. Including those responsible for implementation throughout the consensus process enhances the prospects both of reaching an agreement and of successfully implementing it. Benefits include

- Continuous reality checks: each component of the agreement undergoes an early reality check when implementors take part in negotiations. This reduces the length of the process, since negotiators are less likely to spend time pursuing unrealistic solutions.
- Maintenance of good will: the presence of implementors means that faulty assumptions are identified earlier rather than later, reducing the need to reopen previously "settled" matters, which can lead to disappointment and accusations of bad faith bargaining.

- A wider range of practical options: innovative yet realistic methods of merging interests are contributed by those with practical experience and the responsibility to make the agreement work.
- Less delay: working groups composed of implementors with relevant practical experience reduce delays by helping to identify and prevent problems that can arise during implementation.
- Building confidence in the agreement: when those in charge of implementation help forge the agreement, commitment to and confidence in the agreement are enhanced.

In the Yukon land claims, principal issues were as much as possible taken from the main negotiating table and assigned to working groups composed primarily of relevant line officials and experts representing all parties. Working group proposals formed the foundation of over 30 separate agreements that made up the overall land claims treaty. By involving persons responsible for implementing the agreement in negotiations, practical, workable solutions were developed giving line officials confidence and ownership in the agreement. Line officials who have a sense of ownership in an agreement are more committed to making it work. By dealing directly with each other, they can develop trust and an appreciation for differing perspectives and values. This translates into an invaluable working relationship for managing the unexpected events and difficulties encountered during implementation.

### Building commitment into implementation

Unlike adversarial processes in which either the law or a higher authority binds parties to a process, a consensus process depends significantly on the voluntary commitment of the parties. All aspects of a consensus process should be designed to build and strengthen this commitment. Once an agreement is reached, the relationship among the parties enters a new phase that will continue to depend upon mutual commitment for success.

Each party should consider how it can show respect for the different values and circumstances of other groups and how to signal gratitude for the involvement and contribution of these groups. Some important ways to do this include signing off, final ratification ceremonies, and symbolic first steps.

*Signing off:* Agreements forged through consensus building call upon everyone to sign the agreement. A ceremony to celebrate this signing, accompanied by speeches, group pictures, and gift exchanges, underlines the achievements of the consensus process. At the conclusion of the Sandspit harbour process, a celebratory feast was held at the home of the mediator. For the occasion, the environmental spokesperson had carefully prepared honest and humorous tributes to all the participants, including former adversaries.

*Final ratification ceremonies:* All steps along the ratification journey can be marked by a ceremony. As each party ratifies, others should offer congratulations, privately and publicly. The final ratification ceremony, officially and publicly honouring everyone who made a significant contribution, including people charged with implementation, helps build public and private recognition of the agreement and of its importance. Ratification in this sense is not only an important legal step. It is also a symbolic moment binding all parties to the agreement. Often the emotional commitments can mean as much or more than bare legal commitments; if problems surface later, such bonds will generate the good will essential to ensuring cooperation.

*Symbolic first steps:* When possible, all parties should do something to mark the beginning of implementation. A concrete manifestation of the agreement signifies a commitment that can be publicly acknowledged. In the case of the Yukon land claims, these first steps, which involved all the parties, included establishing local management boards and initiating harvesting plans. This provided an immediate and tangible expression of the reality and benefits of the agreement.

### Creating safety nets

The known realities used to develop agreements change in unpredictable ways, disturbing the balance of arrangements and commitments within the agreement. Consequently, a process must be created to respond to unforeseeable events that adversely affect one or more parties, making it difficult for them to meet their commitments. This "safety net" for the agreement usually takes the form of a contingency plan that sets out steps to follow when unpleasant surprises occur.

Safety nets or contingency plans may include the following techniques: surveillance, mediation, arbitration, and processes for renegotiation. To deal with unforeseen changes that transform fair into unfair obligations, frustrate expectations, generate mistrust, or lead to new disputes as divisive as the original ones, an implementation plan should include a process to revisit provisions of the agreement.

The parties involved in the Northeast B.C. "2005" initiative (described in Appendix 1) put particular effort into designing a set of principles for a process whereby future issues could be effectively resolved.

The inclusion of such a mechanism can preserve the cooperative relationships that have already developed among the parties. An implementation plan that enables parties to continue negotiating and to revise or resolve unanticipated problems bestows several important benefits:

• *Reduced need for detailed provisions:* Excessively detailed agreements take forever to reach; they also involve a rigid attention to detail that can spawn unnecessary disputes over relatively minor issues during implementation. These minor disputes can lead to a progressive deterioration of good will and good working relationships. The existence of a contingency plan to cope with the unexpected eliminates obsession with detail.

• *More confidence in the agreement:* Specifying events that will trigger reviews and framing broad guidelines for reviews can go a long way toward building confidence in the agreement. The knowledge that review processes exist helps dispel fears that come from imagining the host of things that could go wrong.

• *Less time wasted imagining worst-case scenarios:* Processes for renegotiating parts of the agreement changed by events beyond parties' control reduce the need for overly complex contingency plans. Too much time spent on contingency planning can create an atmosphere of distrust among the negotiators and, even more so, within their constituencies.

## Other tools and techniques for improving implementation

A variety of methods can be used to "pretest" the overall feasibility of an emerging settlement. Specialized expertise is always useful. In the Sandspit harbour case, one element of the prospective agreement was the creation of new habitat to replace some that would be lost in harbour construction. Was this feasible and likely to succeed? Although the negotiator from the Department of Fisheries and Oceans was knowledgeable on the topic, he was also a party to the negotiations. By engaging an expert on habitat restoration who had no stake in the Sandspit case, the parties were able to overcome significant barriers to a consensus.

Parties may also employ more direct measures to assess the feasibility of emerging agreements. Role playing and the use of simulated problem solving can give the parties a very direct and immediate sense of what difficulties may lie ahead. Pre-implementation of carefully chosen elements of an agreement enables parties to "test drive" those elements. Pre-implementation measures may involve training, new arrangements for information sharing, or actual infrastructure. Concrete action gives negotiators a learning opportunity while demonstrating tangible progress to those not at the table. In the Yukon land claims, a joint wildlife board was created in advance of the final agreement. Its early work dispelled some parties' fears about whether a joint management board could make competent decisions about complex wildlife resource issues. This experience generated mutual trust and built confidence in the abilities of local wildlife managers and in the viability of the final agreement.

Many other key questions surrounding implementation can be addressed in a carefully crafted action plan: the different ratification procedures needed by each party can be spelled out to avoid confusion and resentment. As well, detailed implementation roles and responsibilities can be defined, as can the consequences for parties who fail to honour their part of the agreement.

Monitoring the progress of implementation is especially crucial. It is all too easy for the parties, having reached consensus, to move on to other issues and challenges. It is essential to include a monitoring system that specifies future targets, standards of performance, and the resources available for monitoring. Appropriate measures for resolving disputes over implementation should be closely tied to a sound monitoring scheme.

## Conclusion

Reaching an agreement is the first measure of a successful negotiation process, but it is not the end of the process, nor is it the most important or most enduring measure of success. Ultimately, implementation is. A "final" agreement is at best a milestone in a long process of continuing work. Negotiations in most circumstances do not end, they merely become channelled into more constructive processes moulded by the experience of reaching and enacting a final agreement. Attention to what lies ahead after a settlement is reached should begin early in any consensus process. This will enable the parties to develop a thorough implementation plan that makes the world a safer place for their agreement.

# Conclusion: Continuing the Process...

*A journey of a thousand miles must begin with a single step.*

— Lao Tzu

This book was written to elaborate on ideas developed by the Canadian round tables on the environment and the economy and published in *Building Consensus for a Sustainable Future: Guiding Principles.* That widely circulated booklet itself built on ideas initially proposed in *Our Common Future,* the Brundtland Commission's landmark report. The Brundtland report argued that local to global environmental problems could not be solved without the cooperative action of all communities (whether defined by geography or shared interests and perspectives). The Canadian round tables' booklet outlined principles for achieving consensus on sustainability issues. The present book is yet another signpost along the way to a more sustainable future.

This chapter recaps the most important and encouraging features of consensus building. It then draws on earlier chapters to present a set of cross-cutting themes, ideas, and advice that, together with the guiding principles, will help parties to negotiate sustainability issues more constructively. Finally, the discussion turns to ways to advance and widen the use of consensus processes.

## The "pros" of consensus

Sustainability is largely about enjoying the fruits of the earth today in such a way that these benefits will be available tomorrow and far beyond into the future. If we did not cherish concern for unborn generations and for the countless other species inhabiting this world, many of today's decisions would be simpler. We would pay little attention to the more distant and subtle consequences of current development projects, enjoying like Aesop's proverbial grasshopper whatever gratifies for the moment. Some believe that, with little exaggeration, this is how modern industrialized and agrarian societies have been making decisions, at least until recently. Many people now recognize that making decisions based on what appears to be immediately "best" and technically feasible is to disregard consequences for other people, other species, and the future.

The importance attached to these concerns varies among the many groups who use or care about the environment. As well, despite several decades of increasingly sophisticated impact assessment, the consequences of development remain difficult to predict accurately. Amid diverse viewpoints and values and unimaginable ecological complexities, it is virtually certain that serious disagreements will abound.

The dangerous result is stalemate and inaction in the face of uncertainty and value conflict. In consequence, the environment is exposed to continuing threats whose extent cannot be agreed upon, while important economic opportunities are hamstrung by doubts and discord. Commonly, "pro-development" and "pro-environment" forces are each powerful enough to frustrate one another's plans, yet both find the status quo unacceptable. The high social and ecological costs of such impasses make it essential to find ways to break stalemates, to move forward in the face of uncertainty. Consensus processes can meet this need. What specifically do they offer in the quest for a sustainable future?

## Meaningful involvement as equals in decisions that affect our lives

Involvement in decision making is meaningful because it is based on a clearly identified commitment and sense of purpose among all parties (Chapter 1); because it is open to all significant interests (Chapter 2) who are participating because they want to (Chapter 3); and because the process is designed by participants (Chapter 4) and can be adapted as circumstances require (Chapter 5).

One of the key and liberating assumptions of consensus is that everyone counts. That is true by definition. If any participant is unwilling to go along with a decision there is no consensus. This means that the views and values of each count equally. And as Chapter 6 pointed out, the commitment to equality goes further. It says that parties must participate on an equal footing, having equal access to the resources needed to negotiate effectively. Otherwise the outcome is little more than coercion disguised as consultation.

## A chance to negotiate and reach agreement on what we know — and don't

Debates and disputes about sustainability are inherently complex. They involve issues about how nature works; how benefits are to be counted; how impacts may cascade through environments near and far and in space and time; what the significance of environmental change may be and to whom; and how, if at all, negative impacts can be mitigated or compensated for fairly. This complexity is often what has enabled parties to hold vastly different views on what the "facts" really are. Through consensus processes, these adversaries have an opportunity to debate and reach agreement on what is known and not known; they can often negotiate a focused strategy for collecting data that can shed light on the issues; and they may fashion adaptive ways of coping with uncertainties that cannot be resolved.

In essence, although consensus processes involve people whose backgrounds may range from casual lay observers to well-known experts on the environment (and economy), such processes recreate one fundamental precondition of good science — direct and open discussion of the facts involving anyone who has an interest.

### A shift from confrontation to accommodation

Most other forums for decision making rely in one way or another on adjudication. This is seen most obviously in the courts but also prevails when administrators make regulatory rulings. The typical "best" approach for stakeholders is to state their case in the most extreme terms in the hope of convincing a decision maker. Consensus instead requires parties to look for common ground in spite of their differences. The very nature of consensus implies that a decision can be reached only when all parties are satisfied. All-or-nothing decisions are not an option. Under this pressure, parties can bring to the table what no judge or administrator ever has: intimate knowledge of what they themselves most need and value.

### An opportunity to (re)build relationships based on trust, respect, and understanding

Sound management of the environment cannot be achieved through one-time deals or decisions. It is a continuous challenge requiring diverse groups to work together despite differing views and values. It rests on relationships, ones that are constructive and ongoing. Again, consensus has a distinct advantage over other means of decision making in this regard. During a consensus process, emphasis is placed on developing a more empathic understanding of other parties (Chapter 7), because without this empathy,

there may be no way to devise solutions that meet everyone's basic needs without offending their basic values. The satisfaction of having co-invented a mutually acceptable solution also contributes to a sound and continuing relationship, as does the contact usually entailed in successful implementation and monitoring (Chapter 10). After a consensus process, parties often find that a simple telephone call can resolve difficulties that previously would have led to open confrontation.

### A focus on "do-able" action rather than high-sounding advice

Consensus processes break with long-standing traditions of advisory consultations and planning. Over the years, Canadians have become progressively more frustrated as elaborate and expensive consultations and inquiries are conducted, impressive reports are produced, and then nothing seems to happen. Or, something does happen but not what the inquiry recommended.

Consensus processes are not like this. They are deliberately directed at devising "do-able" actions and clearly identifying how agreements are to be fulfilled (Chapter 10). The flexibility of consensus processes (Chapter 5) allows parties to fine-tune solutions as needed to implement them. By including everyone who has a stake in making the agreement work, especially those who will be needed for implementation (Chapters 2 and 10), practical and detailed plans can be spelled out.

### Renewing and validating accountability

Consensus decisions are very different from those made in legislatures, bureaucracies, or judiciaries in terms of accountability to people most affected. Politicians must deal with an enormous array of issues, often trading one off against another in legislative bargaining. The bureaucracy is required to be accountable first and foremost to cabinet ministers and only through them to broad publics made of many competing interests. Judges and quasi-judicial panels are quite the opposite, obliged to maintain independence not only from the polity but also from many of the specifics and peculiarities in each case. Their accountability is chiefly to broad legal principles and precedents.

In contrast, negotiators of public policy issues have the paramount goal of protecting and advancing the case-specific interests of those who sent them to the table (Chapter 8). They must, of course, do this with an eye to what will work for other parties. But, otherwise, constituency interests alone dictate their actions and their acceptance of particular solutions and outcomes. This makes accountability far more focused, direct, and uninhibited than is the case for decision makers in conventional dispute resolution settings.

## Recapping the cross-cutting themes

The book has focused on the guiding principles identified by the Canadian round tables. Yet as the discussion unfolded several other important ideas surfaced. Consideration of these cross-cutting themes will further assist those who wish to use consensus processes for sustainability issues. What are these themes?

### Throughout the process: getting started early and going beyond agreement

There is a danger when parties involved in consensus processes focus too exclusively on reaching agreement. Some have called this "agreement myopia." This book has repeatedly stressed how much must be done long before — and well after — the magic moment of signing a consensus agreement. Parties need to take time right from the beginning to define a common objective and to agree on clear procedures of discussion. Consensus groups may find they have deliberately to slow the process down so they can develop a relationship based on trust and understanding. Similarly, parties must look well beyond the agreement, again taking the time to develop sufficient trust and certainty in their roles and responsibilities. This, as frequently empha-sized, especially in Chapter 10, needs to happen throughout the process and not just in the final drafting stages.

### Treating problems in the process as negotiable issues themselves

Often, parties may think that bargaining is only about substantive issues. But creativity, openness to others' ideas, and willingness to talk issues through is equally essential in defining and running the process. This was apparent in Chapter 4, which concluded that self-design by the consensus team can give all parties positive initial feedback on the potential for forging agreement. Similarly, as seen in Chapter 5, ongoing and cooperative evaluation and, if needed, renegotiation of procedural ground rules are essential to maintain the flexibility required by consensus processes, given all the unexpected things that can happen. The same is true after a settlement is reached: the parties must be willing and able to keep talking as implementation occurs, even going back to the table to iron out serious unforeseen problems (Chapter 10).

### Keeping the "world out there" in mind

In several places, this book warned of a trap into which negotiating representatives can easily fall, especially during a protracted consensus process. This is the danger of losing sight of their own constituency and of realities that have remained unchanged away from the table. Negotiators who do this do no one any favours. Without the informed consent and support of their constituencies and a realistic grasp of what can and cannot be accomplished "out there," they are likely to produce agreements that cannot be implemented. It is essential that a consensus-building team remain aware of the ever-changing world away from the bargaining table. In particular, as discussed in Chapter 8, their primary concern must always remain the interests of those they speak for, and they must be proactive in informing and seeking the views of their constituents.

### When NOT to be flexible: defining consensus

One of the best-known virtues of consensus processes is flexibility. Unlike courts and many administrative settings, parties are relatively free to devise rules and options as they see fit. But, as has been pointed out several times in this book, this cannot mean "anything goes." Adherence to a strict definition of "consensus" is critically important. There is a temptation in setting up a consensus process, as well as when concluding the work, to violate consensus principles either by brow-beating minority or weaker parties who have yet to agree, or by simply relaxing the fundamental requirement that everyone agree. To permit this to happen is to destroy the credibility and value of consensus building. As discussed in Chapter 3, it is the significance of the possible disagreement or departure of any party that motivates everyone to try and retry to find solutions acceptable to all. If some coalition of interests believes it can, as it wishes, redefine consensus and exclude those who have different views, it will have little reason to work seriously toward a mutually agreeable outcome.

### Role of the mediator

Several of the examples referred to in this book involved a neutral mediator. Such a presence is not strictly obligatory. Groups of stakeholders can sometimes reach consensus on their own. But as the complexity of disputes and the numbers of parties involved increase, it becomes harder for agreement to happen without someone whose principal and exclusive interest is in seeing a fair and effective process take place. Different chapters have outlined the many distinct functions that a mediator can perform — conducting initial informal discussions to determine whether a process is wanted and possible (Chapter 1); working with initial disputants to identify other key stakeholders whose inclusion is important (Chapter 2); providing general experience with procedural ground rules and ensuring that the parties do not neglect the necessity and opportunity of self-design (Chapter 4); working with the parties to assist them in being effective participants in the process, and thus increasing the likelihood that the process will be effective (Chapter 6). Mediators are in a unique position to act as sounding boards for ideas to be advanced in full group sessions. By attending to the details of meeting logistics and ensuring that progress is recorded, a mediator can help to head off relatively simple problems that might otherwise lead to process breakdown. In essence, by looking out for the details and defending one and only one interest — the integrity of the process — a mediator frees the negotiators to advance their interests in a more determined and effective manner.

## The difficult but essential role for government

The emergence of consensus processes is taking place within an established and complicated system of government involvement and responsibilities. Almost every issue of sustainability is surrounded by myriad regulations and policies. Final say over sustainability controversies rests (and will continue to rest) with elected representatives, and often with the public servants who report to them. On the surface this creates an awkward situation in terms of direct government agency involvement in consensus processes. Government officials may want to stay out of such processes, claiming they need to maintain final and exclusive authority to "rule" freely on an issue. This position is sometimes supported by non-governmental organizations who argue that regulatory agencies have no business "bargaining away" their legal mandates.

This book adopts a different perspective. Without the direct participation of key government agencies, most consensus processes will lack critical information and expertise. Moreover, successful implementation of the resulting agreement will be in question. Without these resources and incentives, other parties' motivation to participate will dwindle. The move toward consensus building has been strongly supported by Canadian governments at all levels because it is a chance for stake-

holders to reach agreement on the most difficult public issues of our time. Government representatives, in coming to the table, are not there to compromise what is legally required of them. Instead, they have an unparalleled opportunity to educate others on the nature and rationale of regulatory policy and, also, to exercise such flexibility as their mandates may already provide.[14]

## Making it happen

Accepting that consensus processes offer important advantages over the more formal and adversarial way of making environmental decisions, what has to happen to increase their use and effectiveness? Despite widespread interest in consensual negotiations, their use remains exceptional rather than the rule.

First, there is a need to dispel some of the misconceptions that surround the "theory" and practice of consensus building.

> *"You can't negotiate when values differ, which is usually the case in environment and development controversies."*

It is frequently asserted that negotiations can only take place over details and when the parties have basic shared understandings and values. No one, it is said, is going to bargain away the things they most cherish and value. So, for example, when a new transportation corridor means increased traffic and hazards to human safety, someone will inevitably say: "We can't negotiate our children's lives."

The response is to ask whether people prefer decisions on such matters to be made entirely outside their control, by judges or bureaucrats. Consensus processes give stakeholders a chance to convey critical values and to explore, with adversaries, ways of protecting these while still accomplishing what these others seek. No one is expected to give up what they most value. In fact, the consensus rule guarantees that no decision will be forthcoming as long as one or more parties feels that their most basic needs and interests are unmet.

Ironically, it is often the case that people with widely differing values are well placed to craft agreements that respect each other's interests precisely because of their differences. One party may care about the fate of a rare species; another may want to build a sub-division. They do not need to spend energy squabbling over why they care about or want these things. Instead, through candid discussion, they can look at options in terms of how well they meet both sets of values. To leave a final decision on such matters to a judge or regulator is to risk one party losing everything or missing an innovative solution that only the parties, by virtue of their intimate knowledge of what they value, could have found.

*"Parties have differing 'power' and you can't negotiate under those conditions."*

Negotiations are unlikely to work if one party has the power to get what it wants unilaterally. Whether this is the case must be assessed prior to undertaking a consensus process. Thus, Chapter 1 in this book concerns the need to determine that every party has a purpose best served through negotiations rather than another avenue.

Consensus processes can actually help to redress some of the inequality in resources that makes one party significantly weaker than others. This was discussed in Chapter 6, as was the point that the decision by seemingly more powerful interests to negotiate with others marks a recognition of reciprocal influence and even empowers the weaker group.

*"Consensus processes just go on and on and on... they're an opportunity to stall."*

Group decisions attract a lot of bad press, especially when consensus is the rule. Typical comments include: "We should just vote and let the majority rule" or "The buck should stop at one and only one point." These views are based on frustration with ineffective consensus decision making. The source of the problem is often ignorance of the preparations needed for constructive collaborative decision making. Simply sitting a group of adversaries down together without due care and planning will usually lead to disillusionment and sweeping generalizations about the ineffectiveness of all consensus processes.

Consensus does take time — although compared with, say, a full adjudication of an issue including appeals, it may not be all that long. But if parties follow the guiding principles, especially when they take the time to establish their own ground rules (Chapter 4), they can accomplish much more than a one-time agreement. Their investment of time and energy pays off in a better working relationship, increasing the odds of successful implementation and of constructive problem solving when the same parties face one another over other issues. By carefully establishing flexible but significant deadlines, as discussed in Chapter 9, consensus groups enhance the prospects for timely and durable resolution of issues.

*"Consensus is compromise and that means solutions are inferior — nothing but the lowest common denominator."*

Consensus is commonly confused with compromise and "least bad" solutions. The Old Testament story in which Solomon proposes resolving a custody dispute by cutting a child in half is sometimes used to illustrate the shortcomings of compromise. But the message of the original story was quite different: Solomon had used a ploy to surface the true feelings and interests of the disputants in a manner analogous to those used occasionally by modern mediators. In fact, in consensus decisions over environmental issues, the resolution is almost never just a matter of "splitting the difference." Usually, many interwoven issues are involved and the challenge is to find creative ways to make everyone better off. As give-and-take options are considered, the parties frequently come to understand each other's interests well enough to devise a settlement from which all can gain.

*"Consensus robs parties of their right to be heard by the courts and/or their elected officials; relatedly, consensus usurps or relieves accountable public officials of their legally required responsibilities."*

Only the most extreme advocate of consensus would argue that the approach should replace all existing institutions and procedures of environmental decision making. In the last several decades important advances have occurred to improve the effectiveness of conventional forums such as courts, legislatures, and administrative agencies in dealing with sustainability issues. In particular, notable reforms have occurred making these institutions more open to public participation and more sensitive to complex environmental data. Consensus processes can further these ends and complement longer-established approaches. If conducted according to the guiding principles described here, particularly Principle 3 — that parties participate

voluntarily — consensus building is always subject to parties changing their minds and pursuing alternative ways of protecting and advancing their basic interests.

*"Consensus presumes trust but there is virtually none when there's been a long and bitter struggle."*

The confusion here is with conditions at the outset of negotiations versus those at the end. At the beginning of a process, no one would sensibly presume to trust parties with conflicting interests, especially when a controversy has been protracted and adversarial. At that point, no one is asked to make concessions or even commitments based on trust.

In the initial phase parties should focus on exploring the pros and cons of negotiations without prejudice to their interests or any obligation to continue to meet. Only when considerable effort has been made to talk about whether to talk and to draft process ground rules, should the parties decide whether to proceed. The process will help engender trust in an incremental manner. The pleasant surprise of finding some common ground with old adversaries and seeing them keep their commitments helps immeasurably. By the time that an agreement is reached, some of its elements may well be based on each party's word. Inevitably, however, settlements provide more formal, even legal, means to ensure compliance. To varying degrees, depending on the case, trust develops through consensus processes: it is never simply assumed.

*"Sure consensus is worthwhile, but we're already doing it."*

Two different, almost opposite responses are commonly encountered when suggestions are made to tackle environmental conflicts with a consensus-based approach. One is: "It won't work here." The reasons given are usually a variation of the misunderstandings already discussed. The other response is something to the effect of: "We're already using consensus — we held a public hearing just last week." The final misconception with which supporters of consensus must often deal is confusion with other forms of public participation that, on closer examination, do not have the core features of consensual negotiations. Broad consultative approaches are not the same as consensus. In consensus processes stakeholders talk directly to each other, not to an authoritative judge or regulator; the purpose is not for each interest individually to stick with its solution but to devise and commit to a single resolution reflecting all interests. Those who want to see consensus used more broadly must take care to make these distinctions when alternative approaches are considered.

Misconceptions surrounding consensus must be cleared away. But other things can be done to advance the use of consensus processes that will lead to a more sustainable future. Much can be learned by reading further in this rapidly expanding field. There are also a growing number of training courses being offered in Canada and elsewhere to help people develop negotiating skills. But, ultimately, there is no substitute for experience through involvement in real-life consensus processes. The question, then, is: how can the use of consensus be increased for problems of sustainability in Canada?

First, each of us can be open to opportunities that come along. A glance through any regional newspaper will usually yield one or more stories about groups struggling over basic questions of how best to use land, water, and living resources. Not all of these will be amenable to multiparty negotiations. But if an increasing number of the people involved are aware that an alternative exists to fighting it out in court, through the press, or by lobbying politicians, the chances are better that consensus will be used. Somewhere, someone will break from the rush into customary ways of dispute resolution to ask: "What if we just try to settle this ourselves?" Readers need to be alert for such opportunities and take the big step (in which there is, in fact, little risk) of initiating a consensus process.

In doing this it may prove worthwhile to invite some assistance, at least in preliminary stages, from qualified dispute resolution professionals.[15] Although mediators must be paid for their help over the course of a full consensus process, many are open to providing some initial advice pro bono, when groups are just talking about whether to talk.

A significant increase in the use of consensus for Canadian sustainability issues will require broader and more systematic commitment than can arise ad hoc through individual advocacy. Already, governments across the country are establishing laws, regulations, and institutions to open doors — and minds — to consensual negotiations. The recent federal Environmental Assessment Act enables government to use mediation as an alternative to full assessment panels, provided that parties are willing. In British Columbia the Commission on Resources and Environment (CORE) has made significant use of multiparty negotiations among stakeholders to develop broad regional land use plans. The National Round Table on the Environment and the Economy has facilitated several major processes of policy dialogue, again centred on the involvement of spokespersons from all key interest groups. In Quebec, in 1993, the formal terms of reference for the Bureau d'audiences publiques sur l'environnement (BAPE) were expanded to recognize the agency's mediating role, a function it had carried out informally for a number of years when convening public hearings on environmental matters. In Nova Scotia, a law has been enacted naming "alternative dispute resolution" as a possibility for a wide range of environmental decisions. Also in Nova Scotia, a bill for municipal amalgamation is in preparation that includes a very specific requirement for multistakeholder processes in solid waste management for the Halifax region. These are critically important steps in ensuring that the opportunity is there, if parties are willing to use consensus building and respect its results.

Canadians have only begun to tap the huge stores of creativity, everyday common sense, and basic good will needed to build a sustainable future. Across the country recognition is growing that not despite but because of our diversity of cultures and perspectives, common ground can be found to accomplish this. Canadians — whether loggers from British Columbia, fishers in the Maritimes, corporate executives in Calgary, Montreal, or Toronto, First Nations in the many homelands, environmentalists working in tiny community groups or internationally known organizations, government officials and politicians at all levels, or millions of others with no clear affiliations — all share important commitments to

- fairness and the goal of protecting the interests and freedoms of all, even those with whom one disagrees,
- an environment that supports Canadians' core values, ranging from economic well-being to spiritual needs, and
- Canadian children, their children, and generations beyond.

These common commitments provide an excellent footing for finding solutions to sustainability issues that are much more than mere compromises, but rather allow everyone to gain. To harmonize the collective action of these diverse publics, consensus will be needed on a multitude of local, regional, and national issues and policies. Groups and individuals require the skill to get along with one another and an understanding of the core principles underlying sound and stable consensus. The present book tries to give Canadians and others with similar commitments to a sustainable future a starting point for understanding consensus-building principles. Now, it is left to them to turn all this talk into action.

# Appendix 1
# Examples of Canadian Consensus Processes

## Western Newfoundland Model Forest Program[1]

*Issues*

The forest resources of Western Newfoundland are critical to the region and the province at a time when the other historical mainstay, the ground fishery, has suffered near collapse. Two of Newfoundland's three newsprint mills rely on timber supplied from the area. The forest is also significant habitat for a variety of mammals and birds. Traditional forest management focused on timber production with little consideration of other resource values.

The Western Newfoundland model forest (WNMF) — set up under the federal government's Partners in Sustainable Development of Forests Program — occupies about 700,000 ha. It is a living laboratory where people representing diverse organizations work together to test and demonstrate sustainable forest management principles and practices.

*Parties*

Each model forest is managed by a team representing principal stakeholders in the forest's future. The management partnerships bring together interests that are often at odds to resolve conflicts and develop the permanent working relationships essential to sustainable development.

The WNMF program began with seven partners and has added others. Original partners include two major forestry companies, government agencies, the city of

---

1   Sources for this case include: Western Newfoundland Model Forest Inc. (WNMFI), Annual Report 1993-94 (Corner Brook, Nfld.: WNMFI, 1994); Canadian Forestry Service, Model Forest Network: Year in Review, 1994-1995 (Ottawa: Natural Resources Canada, 1996); B. Bonnell, "Western Newfoundland Model Forest: A Collaborative Effort in Integrated Resource Management and Sustainable Development," Entomological Society of Canada Bulletin 27(1) (March 1995):28-32; "Western Newfoundland Model Forest Ground Rules," photocopy (n.d.). Information about the program is also available through "gopher files" accessed through the World Wide Web home page:<http://mf.ncr.forestry.ca>.

Corner Brook, an environmental group, and the local community college.

## Process

In March 1993, the team brought in a professional mediator for a four-day workshop on setting procedural ground rules. These rules include conditions for expanding the group, scheduling meetings, and setting up working groups. They also include a section on how to achieve "meaningful involvement" for parties that are not directly involved and for the general public.

From the outset, the partners adopted consensus as their basis for decision making, believing this would be the best way to avoid rekindling long-standing conflicts between interests. A consensus process would ensure no parties felt excluded from critical resource decisions.

## Results

The central operating concept of the program is integrated resource management. This is consistent with the partnership concept that brought the parties together. It means managing the forest for a variety of objectives, including wood fibre production, wildlife habitat, recreation, and wilderness preservation. The challenge is to devise strategies that resolve potential conflicts among uses while maintaining and enhancing overall species diversity and habitat capability.

In its first years of operation the WNMF program has undertaken a variety of activities selected by consensus. Projects range from a seminar and demonstration of horse logging techniques, through mathematical projections of pine marten populations, to operating an educational bus tour. Consensus-based decision making is altering not only forest practices but also the relationships between former adversaries. For example, in spring 1993, logging caused silting of a stream in the model forest. Instead of letting this become an "issue", the WNMF program spearheaded a joint effort to devise and deliver training programs for logging crews working in sensitive habitats.

## Highway Extension at Lévis, Québec[2]

### Issues

In December 1992, the city of Lévis, across the St. Lawrence River from Québec City, proposed development of a new traffic route to ease congestion on its main thoroughfares and create a potential new zone for industrial expansion. In accordance with provincial requirements, the city prepared an environmental impact assessment, which was opened to public review and comment in November 1993. A municipal councillor subsequently raised several serious concerns about the adequacy of the impact assessment and of the highway extension project itself. These concerns related principally to three issues: public safety (the highway would entail a new railway crossing); increased traffic noise on several streets; and impacts on heritage and archaeological resources.

The concerns were directed to the Québec minister of environment and wildlife and subsequently referred to the Bureau d'audiences publiques sur l'environnement

2  The description of this case is drawn from Bureau d'audiences publiques sur l'environnement (BAPE), Prolongement de la côte du Passage à Lévis et réaménagement des accès à l'autoroute Jean-Lesage, Report 74 (Québec City: BAPE, 1994); and BAPE, La Médiation en Environnement: Une Nouvelle Approche au BAPE (Québec City: BAPE, 1994).

(BAPE). The Bureau was originally set up to advise the minister about these sorts of issues and to hold hearings toward that end. Since the early 1980s, however, BAPE has increasingly used mediation to try to resolve environmental disputes referred to it.

### Parties

In this case, the mediation conducted by BAPE was a two-party process involving the municipal councillor (the complainant) who had raised the concerns and the city of Lévis (the proponent), represented by the general manager, the director of technical services, and technical staff.

### Process

BAPE approached the case in three stages. In the first stage (information gathering), BAPE met separately with the project proponent and the complainant to gather general facts about the dispute and to brief the parties on BAPE's role and approach. In the second stage (inquiry), BAPE held more detailed discussions with the parties to explore their positions and ensure all issues had been identified. A visit was also arranged to the site of the proposed highway extension. At the end of this stage, BAPE sought and received approval from the parties to proceed with the third stage — mediation of a resolution.

The mediation consisted of three meetings held over two weeks. The facts were reviewed and suggestions made about how each party's concerns could be addressed. During this time, BAPE also sought input from experts on how to mitigate problems. At the final meeting in March 1994, BAPE laid out a proposed settlement that was accepted by both parties.

### Results

The final agreement included commitments to measures for reducing the project's impact and to further analysis of noise impacts and heritage and archaeological resource issues. The existing plan for the railway crossing was shown to conform to industry standards, clearing up misunderstanding about this issue.

BAPE has used its three-stage mediation approach in a wide variety of settings: other highway construction projects, power plant and transmission line developments, water level problems in reservoirs, and port dredging.

## Grassy Narrows/Islington Mercury Pollution Settlement[3]

### Issues

In 1969, serious mercury contamination was discovered in fish from in the English Wabigoon River system in northwestern Ontario. These stocks were food staples for two First Nation communities — the Islington (White Dog) and Grassy Narrows reserves. The contamination was traced to a pulp mill at Dryden. The health effects were disputed for many years but the economic and social significance of the bands' inability to harvest traditional resources was unarguable.

During the 1970s, social and health conditions in these communities deteriorated.

3  This case description draws primarily on the following articles: A. Campbell, "The Grassy Narrows and Islington Mediation Process," *Canadian Environmental Mediation Newsletter* 2(1) (1987):1-5; R. Blair, "The Grassy Narrows and Islington Mercury Pollution Settlement," *Canadian Environmental Mediation Newsletter* 2(1) (1987):5-9; S.G. Sigurdson, "Settling Environmental Disputes: Reflections of Two Cases," *Canadian Environmental Mediation Newsletter* 2(3) (1987):1-5. Additional information came from A.M. Shkilnyk, *A Poison Stronger than Love* (New Haven: Yale University Press, 1985).

In 1976, when the original owner of the pulp mill, Reed Paper Inc., secured from the province cutting rights to a large uncut stand of timber northwest of Dryden, a heated dispute erupted over the company's role in polluting the English Wabigoon River system. This prompted the creation of a Royal Commission on the Northern Environment (of Ontario). Concluding that action was needed to deal with the impacts on the bands, the Commission recommended tripartite discussions involving federal, provincial, and band representatives. By that time, legal actions for damages against the mill owners had been launched by the bands.

## Parties

Subsequently, the two bands and the federal and provincial governments were involved in two phases of negotiations that took place between 1978 and 1984. Reed, while not a formal party to the mediation, did come to the first all-party meeting in 1979. In that same year, Reed sold the Dryden mill to Great Lakes Forest Products, a subsidiary of Canadian Pacific Ltd. Great Lakes, with plans for a substantial revitalization of the mill and financing assurances from the federal government, required as a condition of purchase an indemnity from the outstanding lawsuit. In the complex negotiation to conclude the sale, an agreement was eventually reached under which the two companies settled on a 50-50 basis liability to $15 million, with Ontario responsible for any amounts in excess of that figure. Neither company participated directly in the first set of negotiations because, in addition to mercury pollution, the first

mediation process included issues related to hydroelectric dams and water level fluctuations. Ontario Hydro was involved in some of the discussions. E.B. Jolliffe, a former member of the Public Service Staff Relations Board and member of the Ontario legislature, mediated the process between 1979 and 1981. When negotiations resumed in 1983, no mediator was appointed but the companies were directly involved.

## Process

The first formal negotiations (1979-1981) failed to deal with the core issue of the bands' mercury pollution claims. The absence of direct participation by the two companies who had successively owned the mill may have contributed to this lack of progress. By 1983, all parties had strong incentives to find a fair consensus on remedial actions. The bands wanted tangible results and help for their people. Great Lakes wanted to bring an end to an avalanche of continuing negative publicity, and closure on a potentially endless string of individual lawsuits. Both the Ontario and federal governments wanted to end an intolerable and embarrassing situation. Negotiations restarted in 1983. In 1984, the parties worked to clarify and narrow down the issues for resolution. Progress accelerated after the appointment of the Honourable Emmett Hall, who had served on the Supreme Court of Canada, as the federal negotiator.[4] In July 1985, the parties reached an agreement that included a mercury disability fund (see below). The agreement was formalized in a memorandum of agreement and ratified by the governments after extensive consultation

---

4   One writer concluded than the role played by Justice Emmett Hall, the federal negotiator appointed in 1985, was "mediator-like...attempting to find common ground between the parties rather than representing the interests of the federal government in a narrow sense." See A. Campbell, op cit.

on the part of the bands. Bills validating the mercury pollution settlement were passed by the federal and Ontario legislatures in 1986.

### Results

The settlement agreement included direct compensation payments. The bands received $16.7 million, of which $11.25 million came from the companies and the rest from the two governments. Individuals with demonstrable symptoms of mercury poisoning were also given compensation. Perhaps the most creative element of the settlement was the mercury disability fund. The negotiators had had great difficulty deciding how future claims would be dealt with, given the possibility that symptoms might not show up until much later in the lives of band members or even in future generations. The fund ensured the bands would be able to meet health and compensation needs in perpetuity and made individual lawsuits unnecessary.

## Saskatchewan Wildlife Diversification Task Force[5]

### Issues

Saskatchewan has had an abundance of wildlife on which rural populations have depended for sustenance. As well, hunting, trapping, and sport fishing have long contributed to the cash economy. The sector has much potential for development but there has been little agreement on how this should proceed in the face of many difficult issues that are raised, such as compensation to farmers for damage done by wildlife, and rapid growth in non-resident outfitting and game farming. Spurred by severe socio-economic problems facing rural communities, the provincial government has sought ways to bring diverse interests together to resolve these problems and find new ways to use wildlife resources. In 1994, the Saskatchewan Wildlife Diversification Task Force was set up to attempt to find a consensus on these issues.

### Parties

The Task Force was made up of 24 organizations. Most were associations representing particular categories of stakeholders, such as hunters, trappers, outfitters, farmers, naturalists, game farmers, landowners, and tour operators. The Métis Society of Saskatchewan also joined, as did several provincial government departments. The Task Force's operating rules singled out non-government members as "consensus members" whose concurrence was deemed essential to the process. An independent mediator facilitated the discussions and process.

### Process

The process entailed 12 formal Task Force meetings between March 1994 and October 1995. Decisions required unanimous consent. The following goals and principles, developed by the Task Force, provided the structure and impetus for the recommendations contained within this report:

---

5   This case description is taken largely from the Task Force's final report: "Saskatchewan Wildlife Diversification: Task Force Recommendations," presented to the Saskatchewan Department of the Environment and Resource Management, November 1995; other information came from the "Saskatchewan Wildlife Diversification Task Force Operating Rules," unpub., April 1994, and from personal communication between author N. Dale and K. Callele, Manager, Resource Allocation, Saskatchewan Department of Environment and Resource Management.

*Goals*

- Examine the options for stimulating economic growth in rural Saskatchewan while maintaining sustainable wildlife populations and healthy landscapes and habitat.
- Recognize and respect the many diverse interests and uses of wildlife while working for the benefit of all Saskatchewan residents.

*Principles*

- Sustainable management of all wildlife resources is a first priority.
- Wildlife is a public resource and property rights in it rest with the Crown, which has ultimate responsibility for its management and use.
- All Saskatchewan residents individually benefit from wildlife and a healthy ecosystem and therefore have responsibility for its maintenance and well-being.
- Saskatchewan residents must have priority access to wildlife.
- Saskatchewan residents must have equal opportunity to access land. Non-residents should not have opportunities to access land that are not given to Saskatchewan residents.
- The legal rights of owners and occupiers of land and any interest in it must be respected.
- The legal rights of First Nations people are acknowledged and respected.
- Healthy landscapes and habitat are critical components of biodiversity and sustainable wildlife management.
- Private landowners and occupiers, as custodians of wildlife habitat, are key stakeholders in development of sustainable wildlife policy.

- Any economic initiatives related to wildlife use should be evaluated against sustainable resource management and sound business principles.

Detailed operating rules were also negotiated early in the process. Among other things, these required representatives to communicate effectively with the diverse individuals and member groups of their associations.

In the summer of 1995, the Task Force drafted and released a discussion document for public review. This was advertised and inserted in its entirety into the *Western Producer*, a widely circulated weekly publication. Subsequently, the Task Force held a final meeting and reached consensus on a document integrating public comments. A final set of recommendations was released in November 1995.

## Results

The final consensus of the Task Force included agreement on guiding principles to be implemented through several detailed recommendations. Recommendations included the establishment of a permanent multistakeholder advisory council; revenue generation through "resource user certificates"; "new provisions to make game farms and 'hunt farms'" more feasible; and a multi-faceted initiative to promote development of ecotourism. The Task Force also explicitly recognized several important areas in which consensus was not currently possible; however, it was able to narrow down and more clearly define issues in these areas.

Provincial agencies are now drafting policy papers on outfitting and concepts such as the proposed "resource user certificate" for public consultation in 1996.

# Alberta-Pacific Forest Management Task Force[6]

## Issues

In 1988, seven projects were announced for new or greatly expanded pulp mills in Alberta. The last and largest of the new projects was a bleached kraft pulp mill to be developed in the Athabasca region by Alberta-Pacific Forest Industries Inc. This project became the centre of acrimonious public debate. Successive environmental impact reviews were held on the direct pollution effects of the mill. These processes were steeped in controversy: the scope was said to be too narrow, the panels ill-chosen, and government was seen to be interfering with the independence of scientific assessment.

In spite of continuing controversy, the Alberta-Pacific mill received provincial approval by December 1990 and construction began the next month. In 1991, the Alberta government and Alberta-Pacific concluded a Forest Management Agreement without a public review, further heightening tensions. The focus of concern now became the manner in which forestry was conducted. The province required a public involvement plan from Alberta-Pacific in finalizing overall forest management planning. Conventional approaches — hearings and community "open houses" — seemed likely to lead to further confrontation. The company asked a professional mediator to help establish a consensus process for forest management planning. The Alberta-Pacific Forest Management Task Force began meeting in early 1992, with the initial objective of setting ground rules for timber harvesting.

## Parties

Great care was taken to ensure all parties with an interest in the case had an opportunity to participate. At the outset, nearly 60 different stakeholders were identified. To make negotiations more manageable, these stakeholders were grouped into five "caucuses": Company — Alberta-Pacific and forest quota holders; Aboriginal — Indian and Métis groups, the Athabasca Native Development Corp.; Environmental/Conservation — for example, Friends of the Athabasca; Resource Users — trappers, outfitters, recreational lease-holders, fish and game associations; Government — Alberta Forest Service, Alberta Fish and Wildlife Service.

## Process

The initial focus for the Task Force was to redesign the operating ground rules for timber harvesting in the Forest Management Agreement concluded between the province and the company. Several full meetings of the Task Force were held in early 1992 to discuss procedures they would follow. In May 1992, agreement was reached on a written set of procedures. Between May 1992 and April 1993, the Task Force held a dozen full meetings and many more subcommittee meetings. By 1993, the Task Force had agreed in principle to new operating ground rules superseding the "bilateral' regulations previously agreed to by government and industry.

To help ensure equality among caucuses on technical and scientific issues, the Task Force

---

6  This case description is based on discussions held in May 1994 with the following representatives of the Alberta-Pacific Forest Management Task Force: Chief Fred Black, Andy Boyd, Bob Cameron, Cheryl Croucher, Jeff Knetman, Mike Mercredi, Doug Sklar, Ken Stashko, and Brydon Ward, and with mediators Gerald Cormick and Joanne Goss.

agreed to a common fund for bringing in experts. This fund, paid for by the company, was available to the Task Force as a whole and also, by agreement of all caucuses, to one of the groups if it felt it needed independent expert advice. In practice, most of the expert input came from the Task Force's own members or staff from the various participating groups.

## *Results*

The Alberta-Pacific Forest Management Task Force can be viewed as a significant and positive break from conventional forest planning and public involvement in Alberta. The resulting ground rules include a much earlier and therefore potentially influential opportunity for public review of annual harvest plans. Significantly, this provision has been extended throughout the province, largely because of the Task Force's innovation. Some other accomplishments include:

- company agreement to suspend forest harvesting in major river valleys pending studies of environmental values and sensitivities,
- all-party support for an Aboriginal traditional land use study to examine special issues related to participating Aboriginal communities,
- a requirement that the Task Force be kept continually informed about harvesting, planning, and fish and wildlife monitoring as Alberta-Pacific proceeds with its operations,
- public input when the company is identifying sites of special sensitivity or complexity in the course of cut-block

planning, and
- identification of key fish and wildlife issues needing further study.

# Sandspit Small Craft Harbour Mediation Process[7]

## *Issues*

The 1988 federal-provincial agreement that created South Moresby National Park promised a harbour at Sandspit, British Columbia. The harbour was intended to stimulate and diversify the Sandspit economy, which had previously depended heavily on timber harvesting in the South Moresby area.

Problems arose when the harbour project, a federal undertaking, came under federal environmental assessment review. The initial review suggested that the harbour site preferred by the community could negatively affect habitat important to fish and overwintering Brant geese.

In the fall of 1991, the parties decided to use mediated negotiations to develop consensus on an acceptable harbour plan. The new federal Environmental Assessment Act provided for mediation as an alternative to full panel review.

## *Parties*

Initially, the process included several environmental and economic development agencies from both the provincial and federal governments, members from an economic advisory committee representing residents of the Queen Charlotte Islands, and an elected

---

7  This case was based on N. Dale's direct involvement as a participant. Other sources included: "Final Report: Sandspit Small Craft Harbour Mediation Process," unpub., submitted to the federal minister of the environment, 1993; and J. Mathers, Sandspit Small Craft Harbour Mediation Process: A Review and Evaluation (Ottawa: Canadian Environmental Assessment Agency, 1995).

official from Sandspit. A professional mediator was retained to facilitate the process. Shortly after the process began, a spokesperson for non-governmental environmental interests joined the mediation group, followed later by a representative of a nearby community concerned about the economic impact of the Sandspit harbour on its own harbour. The Council of the Haida Nation was invited to participate but chose to stay informed on an ongoing basis through regular memos and occasional briefings with the mediator and negotiating team.

## Process

At the outset of the process, terms of reference and ground rules were drafted "to define a commonly acceptable way to provide the community of Sandspit...with small craft harbour facilities...pursuant to the Canada/British Columbia South Moresby Agreement and consistent with the principles for sustainable development and the federal environmental assessment review process." Toward this end, the mediation team undertook a range of activities including meetings of the whole team, setting up specifically tasked working groups, holding informal public briefings, and placing a series of information columns in the local newspaper. The team also sought the advice of experts on topics ranging from waterfowl ecology, through erosion control, to socio-economic impact assessment of alternative harbour sites. The team members' progressively improved understanding of the

issues enabled them to identify two main alternatives to the originally proposed site. These options were discussed at public "open houses" before the parties reached a final consensus recommendation.

## Results

In June 1993, after 14 months, 16 full meetings, many working group sessions and conference calls, and several opportunities for public input, the 15 negotiators signed the "Final Report: Sandspit Small Craft Harbour Mediation Process." This document outlined a site and design concept, identified environmental mitigation and monitoring measures, and set out steps to optimize local and regional benefits of the harbour. The recommended plan was sent to ministers responsible for the South Moresby Agreement and final design work for the harbour began in 1995.

# Skeena Watershed Committee[8]

## Issues

The Skeena Watershed is the second largest producer of Pacific Salmon in British Columbia, after the Fraser River. The life cycle of salmon, their dependence on freshwater for spawning, and their long migration and stay at sea makes them the target of a wide range of users. The challenges of managing this fishery, involving a diversity of stocks with both healthy and vulnerable populations, and a complex chemistry of competing interests

8   This case was prepared using the following sources: Skeena Watershed Committee, "Facing and Forming the Future," unpublished report of a meeting held January 19-20, 1996, in Prince Rupert, B.C.; Skeena Watershed Committee, "Consensus," photocopy, May 9, 1994; "Memorandum of Understanding for the Skeena Watershed Committee Respecting Fisheries Management in the Skeena River," signed February 15, 1992; "Fisheries Management Protocol between the Department of Fisheries and Oceans (DFO)-North Coast Division and the Province of British Columbia," signed June 21, 1994.

had given rise to turmoil, anger, and recrimination. Consensus was reached in 1994 on a three-year framework within which annual fishing plans have been developed and reviewed, and longer term issues associated with the resources and the implications of its management on people within the watershed are being identified and addressed.

## Parties

The SWC is a consensus-based partnership of equals involving five sectors:
- The Department of Fisheries and Oceans (DFO)
- The Province of British Columbia
- The First Nations of the Skeena watershed represented by the Skeena Fisheries Commission
- The Skeena River commercial salmon industry represented by the North Coast Advisory Board, Commercial Fishery Caucus
- The Skeena River sport fishermen represented by the Skeena Watershed Sport Fishermen's Coalition and the North Coast Co-Management Committee of the Sport Fishing Advisory Board.

## Process

The SWC was initially organized in 1992 — after many months of meetings and discussions a Memorandum of Understanding was signed by the parties for the purpose of "fostering communications and cooperation among the parties in order to conserve, protect, and rebuild the salmonoid resources of the Skeena Watershed through a process of consensus decision making."

The initial efforts of the committee met with some success. By 1994 inter-sectoral pressures had continued to build in the fishery, particularly in response to concerns over steelhead and coho and proposed DFO responses. The possibility of mediation to assist the parties was raised through a training/orientation session on consensus-building approaches and options in January of 1994. The parties subsequently requested mediation assistance, and following a period of intensive discussions and meetings, consensus was reached on the framework agreement by late April.

Each of the five sectors has up to six representatives at the decision-making table with wide latitude to include other participants from each sector in the meetings and work of the Committee. A Steering Committee consisting of a representative of each sector and a neutral "Chair" (the term adopted by the parties to refer to the continuing mediator/facilitator role) guides the process between full meetings of the Committee. Several working groups have been mandated to perform specific tasks. A series of workshops have been held focused on specific themes, e.g., selective harvesting, enhancement and habitat restoration, enforcement and compliance. Green Plan funding has made possible an extensive research program, and provided support broadly to the work of the SWC.

## Results

Management of the Skeena fishery has been significantly changed through the SWC — fishing plans and in-season management has taken place in the 1994, 1995, and 1996 seasons within the consensus framework. This all-sector consensus was complemented by a first ever protocol agreement reached in June

1994 between DFO and the Province of British Columbia to provide a basis for achieving more effective coordination for in-season procedures, and to enhance communications and coordination between agencies.

The process has been and will continue to be challenged by deeply felt interests and concerns, complex issues, complicated forces at work in nature, and "big picture" changes taking place within the fishery.

# Yukon Land Claims Settlement[9]

## Issues

Across Canada, efforts have been made to resolve outstanding differences between First Nations and other jurisdictions. In Yukon, unresolved issues included land ownership, jurisdiction over resources and harvesting, revenue sharing, and claims for financial compensation.

After a Supreme Court ruling in 1973 affirmed the principle of Aboriginal title, the federal government recognized the need to settle all outstanding land claims. The Council of Yukon Indians (CYI), an organization representing all First Nations of the territory in land claims, was one of the first groups to submit its land use and occupancy studies as a basis for negotiations.

## Parties

The Yukon land claims settlement affected the interests of a broad array of parties and stakeholders. In addition to the governments of Canada, Yukon, and 14 First Nations, potentially every Yukon resident and all companies based there could be affected. Negotiators from all three principal parties took responsibility for keeping more than 50 interest groups apprised of the process and for ensuring they had input on emerging elements of the final agreement.

## Process

Although the overall process lasted more than two decades, concerted use of innovative approaches to consensus building really began in 1986. Three "ingredients" have been described as key to the success of the settlement process: negotiations training for representatives of the three main parties, followed by training in the communities; extensive use of working groups to bring together government agency experts on specific topics; and extensive consultations with all interests and constituencies not at the table, including regular meetings in small communities throughout Yukon.[10]

## Results

The final agreement was signed by the federal and Yukon governments and the Council for Yukon Indians in May 1993. The agreement provides for a total of 41,439 km$^2$ of land and $242.2 million in cash compensation payable to Yukon First Nations over 15 years. It defines wildlife harvesting rights, subsurface rights, and joint participation on land and resource management bodies, and contains provisions

---

9  The description of this case was developed using the following sources: Government of Canada, the Council for Yukon Indians, and the Government of the Yukon, Umbrella Final Agreement between the Government of Canada, the Council for Yukon Indians and the Government of the Yukon (Ottawa: Minister of Supply and Services, 1993); C. Knight, "Modern Treaty Settles Yukon Land Claims," Consensus (MIT-Harvard Newsletter) (July 1994):1, 2, 4.

10 C. Knight, op. cit.

for promoting and preserving the culture and heritage of Yukon Indians. The agreement is a framework within which 14 First Nations can conclude individual land claim settlements with federal and territorial governments.

# Forest Round Table on Sustainable Development[11]

## Issues

Canada's forests have become a focus of controversy involving many stakeholders. Trees have been spiked, logging roads blocked, and injunctions obtained against protesters in disputes that have attracted worldwide attention. The National Round Table on the Environment and the Economy (NRTEE) was designed to help stakeholders from industry, environmental groups, unions, universities and colleges, First Nations, and government agencies find common ground on significant and controversial environmental policy issues. In 1990, NRTEE set up a Forest Round Table to address forest-related issues.

## Parties

Because of the enormous number of companies, non-governmental organizations, timber-dependent regions, labour groups, and First Nations with a stake in forest management, NRTEE focused on involving existing organizations representing categories of stakeholders. Eventually, 24 organizations agreed to participate in the Forest Round Table. Several companies were also included to bring an operational perspective to discussions.

The process was facilitated by a three-member team: Hamish Kimmins, a university professor of forestry, Steve Thompson, Senior Fellow at the NRTEE secretariat, and John Houghton, a member of the NRTEE.

## Process

The Forest Round Table process began in June 1990. At the first meeting, participants adopted a set of ground rules and agreed on the following objectives:

- the group would develop a common vision for principles of sustainable development in Canada's forests,
- each stakeholder agency would develop action plans for their own contribution to sustainable development, and
- the group would make recommendations to governments and other jurisdictions regarding policies and actions for sustainable development.

The group agreed to operate by consensus, defined as an outcome that everyone could live with even if not ideal from any one viewpoint. The Forest Round Table held nine two-day meetings between 1991 and 1993, and arranged several field trips to give the group firsthand experience of the principles under discussion.

In 1993, the Forest Round Table published an interim report outlining draft principles for sustainable forest management. The following year, work focused on discussing these ideas with member organizations and beginning to devise action plans for implementation. In 1994, the representatives

---

11 Information for this case was based on personal communication in 1995 with S. Thompson, former senior fellow of the National Round Table on the Environment and the Economy (NRTEE), and on S. Thompson and A. Webb (eds.), Forest Round Table on Sustainable Development. Final Report (Ottawa: NRTEE, 1994).

of the 24 participating organizations signed a statement of "Forest Vision and Principles."

## Results

The most immediate result was the statement of "Forest Vision and Principles," which outlined 17 principles under four main topic areas: looking after the environment; taking care of people; land use; and managing resources. The final report of the Forest Round Table[12] sets out commitments made by each party in respect of each principle, and many are now being implemented.

# The Northeast B.C. "2005" Initiative

## Issues

The 2005 initiative was the working name given to a search for ways to improve the effectiveness of the structures and procedures through which decisions are made relating to the exploration, production, and delivery of oil and natural gas in northeast British Columbia. The initiative arose out of a growing sense in northeast B.C. of the need to build a more explicit and effective basis through which agencies, industry, First Nations, local government, stakeholder organizations, and tenure holders could deal with each other. The principal focus of the initiative was on the development of an accessible and inclusive framework for operational and project level planning and a dispute resolution process.

## Parties

The document that resulted, entitled "Memorandum of Understanding Respecting

Operational Land Use Planning for Oil and Gas Activity in Northeast British Columbia," effective July 31, 1996, was formally signed by the Ministry of Environment, Lands and Parks; Ministry of Employment and Investment; Ministry of Forests; West Coast Energy; Canadian Association of Petroleum Producers; and Department of Fisheries and Oceans.

Recognizing the importance of having those anticipated to use the dispute resolution process participate in its development, a workshop was held with participants from all potential users of the process where concepts, approaches, and options were considered. The dispute resolution process adopted builds from those discussions and the sense of direction that emerged from the workshop.

## Process

The 2005 initiative grew over approximately 18 months with different interests coming on board in different ways and times as the need for an explicit set of understandings — or ground rules — to manage relationships and deal with disputes became clearer amongst the various interests and sectors. Process management services, including the delivery of the dispute resolution workshop, were provided throughout by an independent facilitation/mediation team.

An important element built into the understandings reached is the recognition that experience in the use of the process will provide important insight into how it might be improved, and guidance for those using it as to how they might be more effective. To provide the capacity for "learning-by-doing" provision is made for an annual review and a

12 Thompson and Webb, op. cit.

process working group representative of all sectors to make recommendations in that regard.

## Results

The Memorandum of Understanding establishes a framework for the development of pre-tenure operational and post-tenure project planning, information management, and a basis to deal with any disputes that may arise, with the goal of ensuring that those with a stake in any outcome are provided an opportunity for participation so that "whenever possible, final decisions are made on the basis of recommendations supported by a consensus as opposed to being unilaterally imposed."

The Memorandum establishes a dispute resolution process through which the following principles adopted by the parties for dealing with issues and resolving disputes are to be implemented:

- The best way to deal with disputes is to minimize the likelihood of their occurrence through effective communication and planning.
- When issues arise, the parties through the individuals most directly involved should seek to resolve them promptly through direct and active discussion.
- If resolution of these issues is not achieved through these efforts in a timely way, further efforts to bring about a resolution shall be channelled through a clearly defined series of steps with specific triggering actions and time lines identified.
- This dispute resolution process will apply to disputes originating between and among agencies, and agencies and proponents.
- The process is intended to facilitate timely

and effective decision making in the face of differences by providing a basis through which to explore issues in a problem-solving atmosphere, while recognizing the distinct and diverse interests, rights, and mandates that need to be respected, and that statutory decision-making authority cannot be fettered.

- The goal is to attempt to build consensus on a "total package" involving all issues amongst those involved in the dispute by focusing on interests and concerns as opposed to demands and positions.
- It is expected that the committee structure will be used to facilitate dealing with issues and resolving disputes. The parties may wish to consider using specific dispute resolution approaches and mechanisms (e.g., mediation, facilitation, technical task forces, fact finding, non-binding arbitration) in circumstances where it is considered that their use might be helpful.
- So long as the dispute resolution process is proceeding, no steps outside the process should be taken that could affect the issues in dispute without the concurrence of the other parties.
- If agreement is not reached within the specified time lines, the parties will exercise their mandates and perform their roles in accordance with their obligations.

# Appendix 2
# Tasks of a Complex Public Dispute Mediator[13]

U nderstanding the tasks public dispute mediators perform is key to appreciating the competencies they need to acquire. This summary outlines activities mediators conduct. In some cases a mediator will be involved in all three phases of a negotiation. In other disputes a mediator will work on only one or two of the phases listed below.

## Prior to convening the parties

Public dispute mediators may spend weeks to months working with a conflict before the parties are brought together to discuss their differences. Careful preparation is critical to the success of a negotiation.

### Analysing the conflict

Mediators usually assess a conflict to determine what the issues are and whether the issues are appropriate for mediation, what interests must be represented, and whether the

parties are willing to discuss their differences with each other. They conduct interviews with representatives of the interested parties and other knowledgeable individuals and read background materials.

### Designing a process

Mediators are often asked to recommend a process that will enable parties to reach agreements. A process is a sequence of activities that will vary according to the requirements of each conflict situation. For example, a series of facilitated joint meetings may be what is needed for a policy negotiation, while private meetings with each party followed by a joint meeting may be preferable in the settlement of a government enforcement action.

A mediator works with the parties and with the information gathered during an assessment to establish a common definition of the problem, clarify goals for the process,

**13** This summary was developed by the Society of Professionals in Dispute Resolution (SPIDR), *Competencies for Mediators of Complex, Public Disputes: An Overview Developed by the Environmental/Public Disputes Sector,* January 1992.

recommend a general process model, outline specific tasks for the negotiators, and identify interested parties, possible negotiators, and other roles that would be valuable.

### Preparing to post

A mediator must work with the parties to determine how the project is going to be managed, what funding will be necessary and how it will be obtained, invite negotiators and obtain their commitment to participate, prepare a description of the consensus-building process, collect background information about the issues being discussed, and draft and circulate operating ground rules.

## After the parties are convened

Once parties are convened a mediator oversees activities at the table and away from it. Along with negotiation sessions, a mediator may also work with task groups, communicate with individual negotiators, help constituency groups to reach agreements, and provide information to other interested organizations.

### Designing and running negotiation sessions

A primary function of the mediator is to design and conduct negotiation sessions. This includes working with the parties to determine what topics are appropriate for discussion, develop an agenda, and decide on a meeting format. Sessions can cover ground rules parties will use, identifying issues and interests, reviewing information and data relevant to the problem, exploring possible solutions, and drafting agreements. For some of these tasks, facilitation of group discussions will be needed; however, mediation between interests is often a part of this process.

### Promoting and monitoring communication at and away from the table

Public disputes affect a general population, as well as the negotiators. For an agreement to be reached and implemented a mediator must encourage productive communication among negotiators and promote regular and thorough discussions between negotiators and their constituency groups. Progress of the discussions at the table must be understood and agreeable to members of each interest group. When members of one group have difficulty agreeing on a point or strategy, a mediator may be asked for help.

A mediator works with the parties to determine how much and what type of communication is appropriate for the general public and with the media. The mediator can oversee these communications as well.

### Coordinating activities of the different players

Bringing 10 to 30 parties together requires careful logistical planning and coordination. Mediators often arrange the time and the location of the negotiation sessions and notify all participants. In addition to general logistics, the mediator also works with people who serve as resource experts, observers, and the sponsoring and convening bodies to keep them informed and to clarify their roles. More complex public disputes frequently require more than one mediator and often draw on the skills of group facilitators and recorders during negotiation sessions or for task group work. The lead mediator co-ordinates the activities of the mediation team.

### Overseeing requests made and approved by the negotiators

Mediators serve at the pleasure of the negotiators. As negotiators identify tasks, a mediator is responsible for implementing or overseeing their completion. Negotiators may request that information be clarified, appropriate resource people be secured, technical information be collected, or research conducted, and that working groups be set up and staffed.

### Troubleshooting

When multiple parties and complex issues are involved, a mediator expects to do troubleshooting at the table and away from it. Finding ways to reach agreement over controversial data or over an impasse in a draft agreement may require securing more information, identifying a resource person all sides can accept or setting up a task group to handle an impasse outside regular negotiating sessions. Hostile exchanges between two or more parties may require private conversations with individual negotiators and can lead to additional sessions among some or all of the negotiators. For all the problems that can be anticipated, there are an equal number or more that cannot. A mediator must be prepared to handle these problems as they arise.

## Implementing agreements

Agreements reached can be as complex as the issues in dispute and they may take years to implement. Mediators are also retained to help with the implementation of agreements.

### Assisting the monitoring process as requested

Negotiations should include a process for monitoring the implementation of agreements. Monitoring may take the form of a representative group of negotiators meeting periodically to oversee implementation, asking an appropriate agency, especially if it has enforcement powers, to oversee the completion of tasks, or the reconvening of all parties to review current progress. Public dispute mediators can be asked to oversee monitoring activities or be called upon to convene and run particular monitoring committees, helping parties avoid or go around obstacles.

### Assisting with additional negotiations and renegotiations

Agreements vary in their level of specificity. Some carefully define exact substantive outcomes and others suggest procedures that permit parties to continue to work on an issue. Parties that reach a procedural agreement to establish a committee to propose new regulations may ask a mediator to work with the new committee. A mediator may also be called back to renegotiate parts of an agreement that parties later discover are not workable.

# Endnotes

1  Building Consensus for a Sustainable Future: Guiding Principles — an initiative undertaken by Canadian round tables, August 1993.

2  Ibid p. 6

3  Gerald W. Cormick, "Where, When and How to Use Mediated Negotiations: A Checklist for the Potential Participant," Canadian Environmental Mediation Newsletter, York University, Toronto: Vol. 3, No. 1 (1988), p. 7.

4  Society of Professionals in Dispute Resolution, Competencies for Mediators of Complex Public Disputes: An Overview Developed by the Environmental/Public Disputes Sector, Washington, D.C., 1992.

5  A popular maxim in negotiations is "Know your BATNA," the Best Alternative to a Negotiated Agreement. The phrase originated in Roger Fisher and Bill Ury's best-seller, Getting to Yes (New York: Penguin Books, 1981).

6  For several examples of the move toward a consensus-based approach, see Evelyn Pinkerton (ed.), Co-operative Management of Local Fisheries (Vancouver: UBC Press, 1989).

7  One reason for this use is a confusion of unanimity with total satisfaction by all parties: a unanimous agreement is taken to mean one in which everyone is delighted with the outcome. While such a level of satisfaction is not impossible, it is not necessary for unanimous agreement.

8  Canadian Environmental Law Association, Principles for Environmental Assessment (Toronto, October 1973), p. 37.

9  An annotated guide to this literature and other learning materials is available from The Network: Interaction for Conflict Resolution, c/o Conrad Grebel College, Waterloo, Ontario, N2L 3G6.

10  "Active listening" refers to listening for all the cues, verbal and non-verbal, given by a

speaker. It usually involves developing the ability to accurately "play back" what has been heard to the satisfaction of the original speaker.

11 A variety of these tools are described by Roger Fisher, Elizabeth Kopelman, and Andrea Kupfer Schneider in Beyond Machiavelli: Tools for Coping with Conflict (Cambridge, Mass.: Harvard University Press, 1994).

12 The distinction between trustees and delegates has been described by Hannah Feichel Pitkin in her book The Concept of Representation (Berkeley: University of California Press, 1972). See also Sol Erdman and Lawrence Susskind's Reinventing Congress for the 21st Century (New York: Frontier Press, 1995).

13 Under the Canada-British Columbia agreement that established South Moresby National Park, the Canadian government had committed to the creation of a small craft harbour at Sandspit. Subsequently, the provincial government changed, and the fear was that with both of the original governments gone, enforcement of this commitment would be a lower priority.

14 For example, the Department of Fisheries and Oceans' Policy for the Management of Fish Habitat affords many opportunities for cooperative, adaptable solutions to potential habitat problems. These can be best explored through multiparty discussions involving the Department and proponents and opponents of development projects with potential environmental impacts.

15 The Department of Justice Canada will soon have completed a national directory of such professionals including, among others, mediators whose specialty is environmental conflict resolution. Another compilation has been prepared by The Network: Interaction for Conflict Resolution, titled "Dispute Resolution in Canada: Survey of Activities and Services." This is available from the Department of Justice Canada.

# Bibliography

Bonnel, B. "Western Newfoundland Model Forest: A Collaborative Effort in Integrated Resource Management and Sustainable Development." *Entomological Society of Canada Bulletin*, Vol. 27, No. 1 (March, 1995).

Campbell, A. "The Grassy Narrows and Islington Mediation Process." *Canadian Environmental Mediation Newsletter*, Vol. 2, No. 1 (1987).

Canada. Government of Canada et al. *Umbrella Final Agreement between the Government of Canada, the Council for Yukon Indians and the Government of the Yukon*. Ottawa: Minister of Supply and Services, 1993.

———. National Round Table on the Environment and the Economy. *Building Consensus for a Sustainable Future: Guiding Principles*. Ottawa, 1993.

———. Natural Resources Canada. Canadian Forestry Service, *Model Forest Network: Year in Review*, 1994-1995. Ottawa, 1996.

Canadian Environmental Law Association. *Principles for Environmental Assessment*. Toronto, 1973.

Cormick, Gerald W. "Where, When and How to Use Mediated Negotiations: A Checklist for the Potential Participant." *Canadian Environmental Mediation Newsletter*, Vol. 3, No. 1 (1988).

Erdman, Sol and Susskind, Lawrence. *Reinventing Congress for the 21st Century*. New York: Frontier Press, 1995.

Fisher, Roger and Ury, Bill. *Getting to Yes*. New York: Penguin Books, 1981.

Fisher, Roger et al. *Beyond Machiavelli: Tools for Coping with Conflict*. Cambridge, Mass.: Harvard University Press, 1994.

Knight C. "Modern Treaty Settles Yukon Land Claims." *Consensus* (*MIT-Harvard Newsletter*), (July, 1994).

Mathers, J. *Sandspit Small Craft Harbour Mediation Process: A Review and Evaluation.* Ottawa, Canadian Environmental Assessment Agency, 1995

Pinkerton, Evelyn, ed. *Co-operative Management of Local Fisheries.* Vancouver: UBC Press, 1989.

Pitkin, Hannah Fiechel. *The Concept of Representation.* Berkeley: University of California Press, 1972.

Québec.  Bureau d'audiences publiques sur l'environnement. *Prolongement de la côte du Passage à Lévis et réamenagement des accès à l'autoroute Jean Lesage*, Report 74. Québec City, 1994.

———. Bureau d'audiences publiques sur l'environnement. *BAPE, La Médiation en Environnement: Une Nouvelle Approche au Bape.* Québec City, 1994.

Shkilnyk, A.M. *A Poison Stronger Than Love.* New Haven: Yale University Press, 1985.

Sigurdson, S.G. "Settling Environmental Disputes: Reflections of Two Cases." *Canadian Evironmental Mediation Newsletter*, Vol. 2, No. 3 (1988).

Society of Professionals in Dispute Resolution (SPIDR). *Competencies for Meditors of Complex Public Disputes: An Overview developed by the Environmental Public Disputes Sector.* Washington, D.C., 1992.

Stuart, Barry "Land Claim Agreements: A Process for Resolving Resource Use Conflicts." *Managing Resource Use Conflicts.* Ross, M. and Saunders, J.O., Eds. Canadian Institute of Resource Law, Calgary, 1992.

Thompson, Steve and Webb, Allison, eds. *Forest Round Table on Sustainable Development. Final Report.* Ottawa: National Round Table on the Environment and the Economy, 1994.

Western Newfoundland Model Forest Inc. *Annual Report, 1993-94.* Corner Brook, Nfld., 1994.

## Gerald W. Cormick

Gerald Cormick has served as a mediator and facilitator in scores of complex disputes in the United States and Canada. These disputes have involved timber harvest plans, airport noise, urban annexation, tax policies, regulations for pulp mill effluent, and offshore oil development. Mr. Cormick advises governments, non-governmental organizations, and businesses on how to incorporate consensus building and conflict resolution mechanisms. He is a premier trainer in dispute resolution and has developed widely used training materials on the subject. Gerald Cormick, who has a Ph.D. in Business Administration, has served as a professor at universities in Canada, the United States, and Europe. Now at the University of Washington and a principal in The CSE Group, he may be reached by e-mail at cormick@washington.edu.

## Norman Dale

Norman Dale is a mediator and marine ecologist in Vancouver in association with ESSA Environmental Technologies Ltd. He is experienced in multiparty collaboration on coastal zone policy development, environmental impact assessment, community economic planning, and fisheries co-management. He facilitated cross-cultural negotiations on Haida Gwaii/the Queen Charlotte Islands, which led to the establishment of an innovative community trust fund. Norman Dale is co-author of a book on B.C. land claims and has also published articles in both natural and social sciences journals. He has taught planning at the University of British Columbia and studied at MIT/Harvard Public Disputes Program.

## Paul Emond

Paul Emond has taught courses in negotiation and alternative dispute resolution at Osgoode Hall Law School, York University, since 1986. In 1995, he designed and launched the first part-time masters of law (LL.M.) in ADR program in Canada. This was also one of the first such programs in North America. In addition to teaching undergraduate and graduate law students, Professor Emond conducts training workshops in negotiation and ADR for law firms, government agencies and departments, corporations, and NGOs. Professor Emond has spoken on ADR and consensus decision making at national and international conferences. In 1989 he contributed to and edited *Commercial Dispute Resolution* (Canada Law Book), and is currently co-authoring a text entitled *Representing Clients in an ADR Process* (Emond Montgomery Publications, 1996).

## S. Glenn Sigurdson

Glenn Sigurdson, Q.C., of The CSE Group in Vancouver, B.C., advises and works with public and private organizations helping to create structures and systems to manage proactively; to build the capacity to anticipate and deal with issues; and to provide a basis to preserve and enhance relationships in the face of differences. As a mediator, facilitator, and trainer, he has assisted parties in the resolution of complex multiparty disputes in many fields, from fisheries issues to environmental assessments, wildlife diversification to contaminated soil, forest management to right-of-ways, health care to the workplace. He is a labour relations arbitrator and was Vice-Chair of the Manitoba Labour Board from 1980 to 1989. He has written and spoken extensively in the field and has served as the President of the Society of Professionals in Dispute Resolution (SPIDR). He may be reached by e-mail at cse@direct.ca.

## Barry D. Stuart

Barry Stuart, a Yukon Territorial Court judge, was chief negotiator in the Yukon Comprehensive Land Claim. His positions have included Chief Judge, Yukon Territorial Court, and Principal Legal Counsel/Senior Policy Analyst with the Central Planning Office in Papua, New Guinea. Barry has also taught law at Dalhousie and Osgoode Hall law schools. As a founder of Mediation Yukon, the Canadian Environmental Law Association and numerous other organizations, Barry has been active in numerous public issues. He has written and spoken on environmental law, resource management, mediation, consensus decision making, and community and restorative justice. He has taught courses on mediation and consensus processes. Mostly he likes to mediate on rivers while fly fishing.

# Members of the National Round Table on the Environment and the Economy

**Chair**
Dr. Stuart Smith
*President*
*Philip Utilities Management*
*Corporation*

**Members**
Jean Bélanger
*Ottawa, Ontario*

Allan D. Bruce
*Administrator*
*Operating Engineers' (Local 115)*
*Joint Apprenticeship and Training*
*Plan*

Patrick Carson
*Vice-President,*
*Environmental Affairs*
*Loblaw Companies Ltd.*

Elizabeth Crocker
*Co-owner*
*P'lovers*

G. Martin Eakins
*Partner*
*KPMG Peat Marwick Thorne*

Johanne Gélinas
*Commissioner*
*Bureau d'audiences publiques sur*
*l'environnement*

Sam Hamad
*Associate Director*
*Groupe-Conseil Roche Ltée*

Dr. Arthur J. Hanson
*President and CEO*
*International Institute for*
*Sustainable Development*

Michael Harcourt
*Senior Associate, Sustainable*
*Development, Sustainable*
*Development Research Institute*

Dr. Leslie Harris
*President Emeritus*
*Memorial University*

Cindy Kenny-Gilday
*Yellowknife, N.W.T.*

Dr. Douglas Knott
*Professor Emeritus*
*University of Saskatchewan*

Lise Lachapelle
*President and CEO*
*Canadian Pulp and Paper*
*Association*

Anne Letellier de St-Just
*Lawyer*

Elizabeth May
*Executive Director*
*Sierra Club of Canada*

Dr. Harvey L. Mead
*President*
*Union québécoise pour la conser-*
*vation de la nature*

Karen A. Morgan
*Woodnorth Holdings*

H. Joseph O'Neill
*Vice-President*
*Woodlands Repap New Brunswick*
*Inc.*

Edythe A. (Dee) Parkinson
*President*
*C.S. Resources Limited*

Carol Phillips
*Director, Education and*
*International Affairs, Canadian*
*Automobile Workers*

Angus Ross
*President, SOREMA*
*Management Inc. & Chief Agent,*
*SOREMA Canadian Branch*

Lori Williams
*Lawyer*
*Harper Grey Easton Barristers &*
*Solicitors*

**Executive Director and**
**Chief Executive Officer**
David McGuinty